A COMPLETE INTRODUCTION TO
COCKATIELS

A tame cockatiel enjoys human companionship.

A COMPLETE INTRODUCTION TO

COCKATIELS

COMPLETELY ILLUSTRATED IN FULL COLOR

Cockatiels on their playground.

Elaine Radford

Photographs: Gerald R. Allen, 25, 42, 48, 49, 55 bottom, 61, 82, 84, 88, 90, 111. Dr. Herbert R. Axelrod, 14, 21, 26, 39, 66, 68, 102. Horst Bielfeld, 18. John Daniel, 83. Michael Gilroy, 19, 51, 77, 89, 96, 98, 105, 109, 117, 122. E. Goldfinger, 32, 52, 55 top, 56, 120. M. Guevara, 47. Ray Hanson, 33, 41, 46, 69, 112. Ralph Kaehler, 100. Bruce D. Lavoy, 62, 78, 85, 91, 92, 93. W. Loeding, 74, 86. E. J. Mulawka, 27. H. Relnhard, 75. Nancy Richmond, half-title and title pages, 11, 23, 37, 43, 54, 57, 58, 63, 65, 81, 67, 70, 71, 73, 79, 87, 97, 113, 121. Courtesy of San Diego Zoo, 107. Brian Seed, 103, 116. Vincent Serbin, 29, 115, 119. Louise Van der Meid, front and back endpapers. Courtesy of Vogelpark Walsrode, 10, 15, 17, 59. Matthew Vriends, 108. Wayne Wallace, 22, 30, 31, 34, 38, 40, 44, 45, 50, 53, 64, 72, 99.

Distributed in the UNITED STATES by T.F.H. Publications, Inc., 211 West Sylvania Avenue, Neptune City, NJ 07753; in CANADA to the Pet Trade by H & L Pet Supplies Inc., 27 Kingston Crescent, Kitchener, Ontario N2B 2T6; Rolf C. Hagen Ltd., 3225 Sartelon Street, Montreal 382 Quebec; in CANADA to the Book Trade by Macmillan of Canada (A Division of Canada Publishing Corporation), 164 Commander Boulevard, Agincourt, Ontario M1S 3C7; in ENGLAND by T.F.H. Publications Limited, 4 Kier Park, Ascot, Berkshire SL5 7DS; in AUSTRALIA AND THE SOUTH PACIFIC by T.F.H. (Australia) Pty. Ltd., Box 149, Brookvale 2100 N.S.W., Australia; in NEW ZEALAND by Ross Haines & Son, Ltd., 18 Monmouth Street, Grey Lynn, Auckland 2 New Zealand; in SINGAPORE AND MALAYSIA by MPH Distributors (S) Pte., Ltd., 601 Sims Drive, #03/07/21, Singapore 1438; in the PHILIPPINES by Bio-Research, 5 Lippay Street, San Lorenzo Village, Makati Rizal; in SOUTH AFRICA by Multipet Pty. Ltd., 30 Turners Avenue, Durban 4001. Published by T.F.H. Publications Inc. Manufactured in the United States of America by T.F.H. Publications, Inc.

Contents

Introducing the Cockatiel

The demure and winning little bird known as the cockatiel has been steadily growing in popularity ever since the first European explorers returned from Australia with live birds for sale. Today, although it's no longer necessary to trap these free-breeding birds in the wild, more people than ever enjoy the companionship of a pet cockatiel. And no wonder, for a quick look at its many virtues should convince even the most skeptical that a cockatiel comes about as close to being the perfect pet as anything you care to name.

In the avian beauty pageant, the cockatiel may

Above: *Lutino and silver are two of the color varieties not found in the wild but fostered in captivity by cockatiel breeders.*

win no prizes for flashy feathers like its smaller rival, the budgerigar, but its agreeable personality more than makes up for its subdued coloring. Gentle and easygoing, it happily befriends its human owners, eagerly looking forward to playtime spent with you and often calling for your attention with a peremptory "peep." Because it's both easygoing

The wild, or normal, coloration of the cockatiel is gray. Genetic mutations alter the pigments visible here.

and relatively small, the cockatiel is one of only two commonly kept parrots—the budgie is the other—that can be safely cared for by children. And because it's hardy as well as smart and eager to please, you'll enjoy its company for many years to come. Although 12 to 14 years is more likely, a few ancients have lived over 20 years.

Still, it doesn't matter how sweet your pet is if the landlord or neighbors won't have it around, as many dog and cat owners have learned to their sorrow. Fortunately, the cockatiel is also well suited to apartment and condominium living, and few people will ever have cause to complain even if they're aware of your pet's existence. Although the cockatiel's cry can be insistent, it isn't especially loud or irritating, so noise isn't a problem. "Messiness" shouldn't be a concern, either; like all seed-eating birds, cockatiels are extremely neat in their habits. Even if you don't succeed in potty training your bird to defecate only when in its cage, you'll soon notice that when it's free it always flies to a few favorite positions around the house. Once you fix these spots up with paper or washable fabric, you'll be able to keep your home clean while letting your pet get its exercise.

Finally, cockatiels are one of the few easily bred pets that yield offspring of value.

We're all aware of the dog and cat overpopulation problem; their young often cannot even be given away, meaning the offspring end up abandoned to starve and spread disease—and the problem will only get worse as more people move into multi-family dwellings. Birds, on the other hand, are growing in popularity; if you or your children want to raise some cockatiels, you can do it safe in the knowledge that healthy, reasonably priced offspring will always find a buyer. Furthermore, cockatiel breeding is excellent practice for parrot breeding in general, a wonderful enterprise for any bird enthusiast concerned about the status of the many vanishing species of parrot in the world.

Life in the Wild

By happy coincidence, its life in the dry Australian interior has helped make this congenial bird the agreeable little pet it is. *Nymphicus hollandicus,* as scientists the world over call the cockatiel, is a nomadic inhabitant of a continent that seems designed to produce pet-quality birds. Because rain may not fall in one region for months or years cockatiels must travel in flocks in search of water. Pairs can't settle down to nest at regular, predictable intervals, but must instead be ready to raise young whenever the drought happens to break. As a consequence, the cockatiel is

The cockatiel as depicted in
Greene's Parrots in Captivity
(1884–87).

Above: *Among the birds kept as pets, the cockatiel is one of the species that does best in the artificial habitats of cages and aviaries.*

a good-natured, sociable bird that gets along well with other members of its nomadic flock, as well as a tough survivor that can be ready to breed at practically the drop of a hat! In captivity, your family becomes the cockatiel's flock, and you will soon notice that your pet thrives on the kind of constant attention it would have received from its companions in the wild. Incidentally, it's interesting to note that the same environment has shaped two other popular and personable avian pets, the zebra finch and the budgerigar.

Unlike many parrots,

cockatiels do most of their feeding on the ground, foraging on ripening grasses. Hence their natural reaction to being startled is to fly up, leading to their infamous skill in colliding with windows and ceiling fans when frightened. You'll also notice that your cockatiel seldom or never holds its food in its claw like the parrots evolved to eat sizable morsels such as fruit and buds will do. Both behaviors are sometimes mistaken for evidence of low intelligence in the cockatiel, but they're actually perfectly normal adaptations to their special environment.

In the wild, all birds of a single species tend to look alike, and cockatiels are no exception to the rule. The gray, or normal, variety with the long white wing bars has the same coloring as that seen in wild birds, a quietly attractive plumage that helps it blend into the background when sitting on its favorite wild perch, a dead tree. If a predator does dive into a flock, the fact that all the birds look much the same can prevent the attacker from focusing on a single individual and chasing it to exhaustion.

A troublesome problem for breeders of most parrots is that you can't easily distinguish males from females by eye, causing one vet to write that the number-one reason for parrot-breeding failures is people misjudging the sex of their birds! Fortunately, the agreeable cockatiel hasn't taken the lookalike principle to this extreme. Adult males and female are very easy to sex once you've seen a pair together—the males are the ones with the much brighter yellow heads and prominent orange cheek patches. However, since the brilliant male plumage doesn't appear for six to eight months, young birds are quite difficult to sex.

The Domestic Varieties

In captivity, of course, cockatiels don't have to worry about predators. If a mutation (genetic change) occurs that affects a cockatiel's color, it can still grow up to raise babies of its own and pass on the new color trait. Therefore, breeders have been able to capitalize on such beneficial changes to develop many beautiful varieties of colored cockatiels. However, you will probably never have the rainbow of choices that you do with budgies because the basic cockatiel pigments are red, yellow, and black. The gray feathers, for instance, result from a mixture of black and yellow pigment, while the orange is a mixture of red and yellow. White feathers contain no pigment at all. With this limited palette, even the most artistic breeder isn't likely to ever come up with a, say, leaf-green cockatiel because such a development would require more than a change in how cockatiel pigment is distributed on the body; it would entail the appearance

Above: *A handsome heavily pied male cockatiel.*

of a new pigment altogether. Expecting such a change is comparable to hoping that someday a human baby will be born with naturally fuchsia hair.

The first mutation noticed by breeders was a splotchy-looking variety called the pied. Pied cockatiels have white and yellow spots on their body wherever they lack black pigment, often giving them an absurd "harlequin" appearance. "Heavy pieds" have more than 50 percent white and yellow feathers, while "light pieds" can have much less—perhaps only a few out-of-place white and

The Domestic Varieties

yellow feathers scattered about normally gray areas of the body. The ideal pied would have symmetrical body markings, but that almost never happens! Since it's more amusing-looking than beautiful, the pied never really caught on as a pet. Most breeders also pass on the pied, having learned that there is no way to predict the appearance of the young. Heavy pied parents may produce light pied offspring, and vice versa—and every chick in the bunch may turn out to have lopsided, asymmetric coloring.

In contrast, the second mutation developed with human help turned out to be the most popular of them all, the lutino. Lutino cockatiels lack black pigment, so that they have no gray or black areas on their bodies. Because the yellow pigment is still present, these birds are *not* true albinos, although some people mistakenly refer to them as such. The head is usually a particularly attractive deep yellow, and the orange cheek patches of both sexes are a deep, brilliant color untinged with gray. As it turns out, the female is not only as beautiful as the male in this incarnation, she is usually a richer, deeper yellow than her mate. Besides the gray, this is the variety you're most likely to meet in pet stores.

Depending on where you live and shop, you may encounter one of several

Below: *Cockatiels range over most of the Australian subcontinent.*

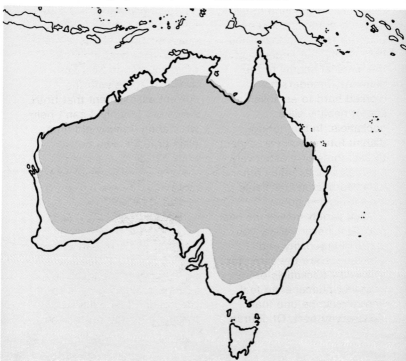

other attractive varieties. The true albino mentioned above is an all-white cockatiel with no cheek patches: some people say it resembles a tiny cockatoo and expect it to become a popular pet as soon as breeders can make more available to the public. The opaline, or pearled, cockatiel is especially lovely because each affected feather is white or yellow with a dark gray border, giving the bird a rich, scalloped look. (Unfortunately, adult males molt back to normal gray plumage, so only females retain the beautiful coloring for their entire lives.) In cinnamon cockatiels, the black pigment has turned brownish, giving the birds an attractive tan color. Silver cockatiels are a pale silver instead of the usual gray due to a partial reduction in black pigment. Early specimens suffered from blindness and low fertility, but because of the unusual beauty of the plumage, breeders have worked hard to establish a line of healthy silver cockatiels. In the not-so-distant future, you can expect to see some of these lovely birds as well as many other varieties become available to the bird-loving public.

What variety makes the best pet? Whichever variety you prefer! Personality and intelligence are the same for all healthy cockatiels of whatever plumage, so feel free to pick the one that pleases you best. Of course,

Above: *In Australia, wild cockatiels are often observed perched on telephone lines.*

the more attention it gets, the happier and more playful it becomes, so a "prettier" bird is bound to seem smarter if its looks win more of your attention. In this light, it's interesting to note that older books often disparage the pet qualities of female cockatiels, while books written since other mutations became available agree with the current assessment that both sexes are friendly. I can't help wondering if many old-time plain gray females became poor pets because their owners unconsciously gave more affection to their prettier mates. Now, in some varieties, it's the male who might get shortchanged in the attention department! In any case, since the difference in price between the lovely lutino and the ordinary gray is small, you needn't feel guilty about springing for the prettier bird.

17

Choosing Your Cockatiel

Because it's a living creature, a cockatiel shouldn't be purchased on impulse. Before you commit yourself to the responsibility of keeping an animal, you should take a long look at your current lifestyle. Parrots in general and cockatiels in particular are social birds that expect to become part of the family when kept as single pets. Do you honestly have time to

Above: *Normal, silver, lutino—these varieties show the extent to which pigmentation is diluted in the cockatiel.*

spend with your bird every single day? Unless you do, your naturally gregarious pet will become lonely and possibly neurotic. An unhappy dog may mope, but an unhappy bird dies. It's

This color variety combines the pearl and the cinnamon mutations.

unfortunately not rare for a depressed bird to mutilate itself or even to commit suicide by tearing out its own feathers! If you party or travel a lot, you probably don't have time for a single pet cockatiel. Perhaps you could get a pair instead; although birds that amuse each other will never be as attentive to *you,* you'll know that your pets' psychological health is secure even when you can't dote on their every wing-flap.

Before purchasing a cockatiel for a child, do make an honest assessment of the youngster's interest and abilities. Even a mature child may be too active to pay much attention to a cage-bound pet. In my opinion, it's better never to give a pet parrot as a gift, although a pair of small finches may be perfectly suitable. However, a cockatiel is expensive enough that a child who has saved up his or her own money probably has a genuine interest that will be richly rewarded by the pet's gentle admiration. In that case, it would be a nice move for you to spring for the cost of the cage.

You should also consider how important it is to you to have a talking bird. Cockatiels, like all parrots, have the ability to learn to talk, but in practice they rarely do. The more inexpensive budgie is actually a far better talker in terms of vocabulary; it's possible for some specimens to utter hundreds of words. Large parrots, on the other hand, might not say much, but what they do say is clear and human-sounding. Cockatiels are neither particularly talkative nor especially easy to understand. If you know in your heart of hearts that you'll be disappointed if your pet never learns to speak, seriously consider buying another kind of parrot. Yes, there are exceptions, but in most cases you'll find that the owners of talented talking cockatiels have an unusual amount of time to spend training their pets.

A final consideration concerns you and your family's health. Feathers aren't irritating to most people unless they sleep on a pillow of them, so most parrots kept in clean cages aren't anywhere near as allergenic as a pet cat or dog. However, the cockatiel, like its larger cockatoo relatives, *may* aggravate some allergy-prone individuals. The reason is that these birds shed a white dandruff-like powder called "cockatoo dust." Most people won't be bothered by the dust if they mist their pets with a light spray each day, but if a family member has severe allergy or asthma problems you would do well to consider buying a budgie instead. It wouldn't hurt to ask the allergist. In my case, I can attest that despite my severe house-dust and animal-dander allergies, my doctor correctly predicted that bird

Cockatiels, unlike some other parrot species, do not have any strong odor.

keeping wouldn't create any problems.

Choosing Your Bird

All things considered, you'll probably find the cockatiel a terrific choice if your schedule and respiratory system allow you to keep a pet at all. The next step is the enjoyable chore of shopping around. In most areas, a check of the Yellow Pages and a major newspaper's classified section will yield several potential sources of cockatiels. Unless you've got your heart set on a rare type like an albino, you should

Below: *Cockatiels most easily become tame if they are accustomed to human contact while still young.*

have your choice of healthy, young pets, so take your time and look around. If you have the tiniest doubts about a particular specimen, keep looking. You'll find the one you want sooner or later, probably sooner.

The first thing you'll notice is that you can easily buy cockatiels both at pet stores and from private breeders. Both sources have their advantages. The pet shop will often accept credit cards, and it will certainly have suitable cages and other supplies for sale. The breeder, on the other hand, will be able to give you a better idea of the bird's background, possibly even showing you your pet's parents. Breeders are also more likely to have special mutations and "show" quality birds, although you may have to do some begging and pleading to coax a special specimen out of them.

If you decide to buy from a breeder, go to the pet store and buy the cage first. The cage can wait for the bird, but the bird shouldn't have to wait for the cage.

Choosing the right bird is a process that starts when you walk in the door, whether it's a private home or a shop in a busy mall. There is never any reason for a cage of cockatiels to smell; if any seed-eating birds or their cages stink, then the store or aviary isn't clean enough. Although wastes are going to accumulate in the cage bottom during the course of

Above: *Normal, pearl, and pied are some of the varieties readily available for purchase in pet shops.*

the day, they should be scent-free. Perches and dishes shouldn't be caked with feces, either. Because it's a temporary situation, some sellers will display several cockatiels to a cage, but they shouldn't be crowded in so closely that they have to sit pressed against one another. (Some birds like this. Cockatiels don't.) But you won't have any trouble eliminating overcrowded aviaries from your list. The broken feathers and irritable

dispositions of the avian inhabitants will do that for you.

It's also a good idea to ask about the seller's policies. Many pet stores will sell you a cockatiel with a written guarantee that you may return it if it doesn't check out healthy with your vet. Cockatiels aren't costly, but they are expensive enough to warrant a post-purchase exam if you have this option. A small breeder might not be able to offer a guarantee, since his or her business isn't large enough to absorb losses from even the occasional crackpot customer, but the smaller operation is less likely to have been exposed to avian disease. Use your judgement.

Anatomy of a cockatiel: the bones associated with the limbs are colored blue.

If you want a breeding pair, you should start with an *adult* male and female so that you can be sure that's really what you're getting. With a household pet, however, you should try to get the youngest cockatiel you can that's ready to leave the nest. Don't worry about the fact that you can't tell yet whether it's a girl or boy; it won't make any difference in the pet quality of the bird. It's far more important that you start taming at an early age. If you're bothered by calling a family member "it," you're welcome to guess at the ultimate outcome. But since you'll probably guess wrong— at least, *I* always do—give it an androgynous name anyway!

How to determine age? To a certain extent, you'll have to trust the breeder or pet-shop clerk, but there are certain signs of youth you should look for. Juveniles quickly reach adult length, but they're often noticeably more slender than older birds. Fledglings less than two or three months old have pinkish rather than grayish bills. Until they're at least six months old, the whole brood will resemble females in their coloring, except that the pale stripes on their chests will be *more* prominent than in the adult birds. (This is unusual because in most bird species, juveniles have less distinct patterning than adults of either sex.)

Some breeders can offer handfed birds, that is, birds that don't have to be tamed because they were raised by human hands. Some people say that the cockatiel is so naturally loving that handfeeding's a waste of time, but most agree that these specially pampered babies make the smartest and most affectionate pets of all. Especially if you've never kept a parrot before, the knowledge that your new pet is already tame can be very reassuring! Since they seem to consider themselves tiny

Below: *This young cockatiel, probably a male, is four weeks old.*

humans, handfed cockatiels are also the ones most likely to learn to talk. Of course, you must expect to pay extra since human rather than bird labor went into raising these sweetheart specimens.

Before buying any bird, you need to give it a visual health exam. Unless your name is Rockefeller (and you don't

even alarm, when you draw near. A bird that just sits and looks at you may be tame—or it may just feel like it's beyond the point of caring. If it's puffed up to keep warm or sleeping on the floor rather than up on its perch, it's definitely not feeling up to par. Of course, most birds siesta in the early afternoon, and a

have any other birds at home), I suggest that you make it a rule never to take in a sick bird because you feel sorry for it—not even if it's being given away for free. The additional stress of moving from shop to home is more likely to kill the cockatiel than to save it, and if you do have other pets, you run the risk of bringing a disease home to them.

Watch how the cockatiel behaves when you approach its cage. If it hasn't been handfed or otherwise tamed, it should move about and show some signs of alertness,

Before choosing a cockatiel for a pet, take time to observe the individuals available. Before long, differences in temperament among the birds will become apparent.

very calm specimen may manage to catch a snooze even in the midst of the noon rush, but at the very least it should be dozing normally, sitting on its perch with one foot drawn up near its belly, and it should certainly open

While the cockatiel you intend to purchase is in the hand, examine it closely for signs of illness.

an eye once you start talking to it.

All body openings, including the vent, should be checked for abnormal discharges. When the seller catches the bird for your attention, ask him or her to turn the bird over so that you can make sure that there are no caked feces blocking the vent. Any fluid around nostrils, eyes, or vent is cause for rejection. Also check the condition of the plumage. It's okay if a rambunctious cage partner pulled out a wing or tail feather; those grow back pretty quickly. But only a sick or depressed bird fails to keep what feathers it does have spotless.

Acclimating the New Cockatiel

Meeting a bunch of new people is stressful even for a tame cockatiel, and it's doubly hard on an untamed one. To get off on the right foot, you want to make sure you have the proper cage waiting in the proper spot. A light, comfortable, draftfree room where the family members spend a lot of time is best. Unfortunately, the kitchen is out, even if it is the center of your home universe. There are just too many overwhelming fumes produced here that can irritate a bird's delicate respiratory system. Incidentally, natural gas is especially bothersome, so don't put the cage near any gas heaters or stoves. By

contrast, a cozy den or TV room is usually a great place for a cockatiel, who will be happy to prance from shoulder to shoulder diverting your attention from the latest network idiocy. Of course, if the cockatiel isn't tame yet, you should start with a quieter spot and work up to introducing your pet to the family circus.

Before you plop down the cage, check the proposed position for drafts. Locate any vents and make sure no air, either hot or cold, will be blowing on the bird's cage. A candle test will quickly tell you whether a particular spot is safe for a cockatiel; if the flame doesn't waver or flicker, you've found a draftfree position.

When you place your new cockatiel in the cage, be sure to talk to it in a reassuring tone. Because it may feel disoriented and confused, it may not be up to looking around for the food and water dishes, so have some seed scattered on the floor of the cage where the ground-feeding cockatiel naturally looks first. No doubt everyone will want to hover over the cage to welcome the newcomer, but take it easy and give the bird a rest after its journey. Tell the kids to whisper, not shriek, their delight. The cockatiel will be in the rough-and-tumble of family life soon enough, far more quickly and easily than you'd ever housetrain a new puppy.

Since a pet cockatiel will spend a great deal of time in its cage, be sure that you choose a suitable cage and select its location carefully.

Your Cockatiel's Home

Above: *The principal furnishings needed in a cockatiel's cage are perches and feeding utensils. The wire top of this cage can be detached from the base, making cleaning easy.*

Many people have such a bad attitude toward cages that I wonder if they think "cagebird" and "jail bird" mean the same thing. Actually, all parrots tend to think of their cages as their homes unless the accommodations are truly dreadful. If the roof's constructed for comfortable perching, you'll probably soon notice that your pet enjoys spending a good deal of time playing on the top of its cage. The security of knowing food and a safe retreat is near is as nice as the freedom to visit you or to flap around the room for some exercise.

Cages also protect your bird when you can't be there to supervise. Let's face it: The average home is a disaster waiting to happen when a small flying creature is free to spend eight working hours a day looking for trouble. The tragic accidents that commonly befall cockatiels include drowning in a half-full water glass or open toilet bowl, eating a delicious-looking but poisonous houseplant, and taking off out an open door when you come home. A serious accident can also befall your furniture—that little snub beak is a lot more damaging than it looks. And if you have other pets loose in the house, the possibilities are endless. A cockatiel cage, therefore, is a necessity, not a luxury.

Three considerations will dominate your choice of a cage: size, chew resistance, and ease of cleaning. The most important factor is size. The cockatiel must have room to play with its toys and putter around when it's left alone. They seem to like games of climbing up and sliding down, and flipping beak over tail around a perch, so a *tall* cage is better than a long one of the same volume. As a minimum, it should be wide enough to let the cockatiel spread its wings without brushing the sides. Good dimensions for a pair or a single bird are a foot and a half to a side and at least two feet of height. Although this suggestion constitutes an absolute minimum for a *pair*, I don't advise going much smaller for a single bird. It will need the room for extra toys and such, and besides, since cockatiels can be bred without sacrificing their pet qualities, you never know when you might get the urge to breed your bird.

Large cages do cost significantly more than small ones, and the cage might well cost more than your pet. It's worth it, though, in the increased life expectancy and happiness of your cockatiel.

These birds aren't happy sitting like bumps on a log all day; they need room to stretch and play. Without it, they can get fat from spending too much time eating and not enough exercising, and the resulting obesity can lead to a host of physical ailments. More likely, the bored bird will start tearing at its own plumage or simply mope itself to death. Only one of a kind of bird belongs in an antique or designer cage just big enough to turn around in place—the ceramic kind! Unless your

Below: *A door hinged at the bottom makes a convenient landing perch for the cockatiel to enter or exit.*

cockatiel is injured or ill, its cage really can't be too big.

The cage should also be able to stand up to the cockatiel's relentless beak. Unless you want to build a new cage every few months, that means a metal, not wood, frame. Plastic trim is okay, as long as it's where the cockatiel can't chew it off. If you must have a bronzed or painted cage, please buy it from a reputable *pet* supplier, not from an antique dealer, department store, or somebody's granny's attic. The pet dealer's offerings may not be as glamorous but they'll be safe. Ritzy brass and pseudo-brass creations, by contrast, are sometimes put together with lead solder, a deadly poison to pet birds. Cages painted by people with no bird knowledge may even be completely coated with poisonous lead-based paint! If

you must have a cage that matches a particular color scheme, then have it painted yourself with a lead-free paint safe enough to use in a baby's crib. Read the labels. The safe products will be happy to tell you about it.

At the other end of the spectrum are the people who don't give a hoot *what* the cage looks like, as long as it's cheap and homey for the bird. If that's you and you're handy, you can build your own simple rectangular cage from sturdy hardwire cloth, joining the sides with strong poultry staples. Be very careful to

Below: *In additional to nutritional value, a cuttlebone offers the cockatiel an opportunity to exercise its propensity for chewing.*

check your creation for rough edges, and file down anything that could catch a tender foot. It won't be fancy, but the cockatiel will think it's a castle—especially if this arrangement allows you to buy your pet some extra room.

A final question: how easy will it be to clean the proposed cage? For cockatiels, I like the cages with pull-out trays that can be whipped out in a flash for a change of paper. However, such cages really should have a bottom screen to prevent your pet from munching on newsprint. It can't be one of the deadliest poisons, since all parrots seem to grab a taste of the daily news sooner or later, but it has been known to kill some individuals. If the cage bottom lacks a protective screen, you may prefer to keep the tray filled with corn-cob or wood-shaving litter. Good litter can go two or three days between changing, but the trade-off is that each change is a bit harder to make.

Should you cover the cage at night? You shouldn't have the cage in a spot where covering it is absolutely necessary to protect from cold drafts or blasts from the heater, but it is valuable to cover the bird to give it some quiet, especially if some family members are night owls. A cover also discourages late visitors from pestering a pet who's trying to sleep. Bear in mind that your cockatiel likes

Above: *A cockatiel kept singly should have its cage situated in a room where it can observe family activities.*

routine, though; it will want to be covered every night, not just the evening of the big party.

Perches, Toys, and Playpens

Other than the food and water drinkers, the most important item of "furniture" in your cockatiel's cage is its perches. Most cages will come with perches already supplied, but you'll need to get extras anyway. Plastic perches should be replaced immediately since they aren't very comfortable for the

cockatiel's feet and don't keep its nails in trim. The wooden kind which do provide comfort for feet and exercise for beak get chewed up sooner or later. With luck, your cockatiel cage will come with the right size perch for your pet's feet, but if not, the pet store probably has a nice selection of more appropriate perches. If you have the choice between round, oval, and square perches, great. Take one of each so that your bird won't always have to grip the same way. You should also make sure that the diameter of the perch is wide enough so that the toes don't wrap around on top of each other, but not so wide that the bird can't get its claws three-quarters of the way around it.

Nice, natural perches are even better, and the price is certainly right when they come from your own back yard. Twigs and small limbs from birch, willow, and fruit

Above: Perches of various diameters promote the exercise that prevents foot problems from occurring.

trees are great for chewing as well as perching. The main drawback is that you must be sure that the tree hasn't been sprayed with insecticides for several years since such chemicals are, after all, poisons that can weaken or kill a small bird. Unfortunately for the urban dweller, spraying isn't always under your own control. Down here in New Orleans, for instance, it's necessary for health reasons for the city to spray neighborhoods regularly to combat mosquitoes. Any front-yard peach tree is sure to absorb at least a little of the insecticide. But if you *can* give your cockatiel a fresh, green twig for perching— flowers and all—your pet will get vitamins, exercise, and good clean fun from slowly chewing its new perch to smithereens.

An occasional problem with employing natural perches that have been previously used by wild birds outdoors is the chance of a red-mite infestation. These tiny creatures hide in aviary crevices during the day, creeping onto a bird to suck its blood at night. Therefore, if your bird has been scratching and fidgeting a lot, you should check for red mites by waiting until nightfall and covering the cage with a white cloth. The blood-filled mites will show up as mobile red dots fleeing the bird when you turn on the light. Fortunately, the horrid little things are quite easy to get rid of. Many safe mite sprays are available in pet stores for using directly on birds. To prevent re-infestation, thoroughly clean cage, perches, nest boxes, and toys and then dust with a pet-store mite treatment or a little Sevin dust mixed with talcum powder. One treatment is usually enough. Better yet, you can probably avoid the whole problem by using the small hanging "bird protectors" that guard against mite invasion in the first place. Just don't forget to replace the protective disk at the recommended intervals.

Don't overcrowd the cages with perches in your enthusiasm. Too many perches prevent your pet from moving freely and hence obstruct the very exercise and comfort you're trying to provide. A couple of perches is plenty for the usual home cockatiel cage. Be sure to position them in such a way that the cockatiel can sit without defecating into the food and water drinkers. Such accidents aren't just unsightly; they're a threat to health.

All parrots love toys. Mainly, they love to eat their toys. Because chewing is excellent exercise for keeping its beak in trim, expecting your cockatiel to treat its toys nicely or do without is impractical. Give the fact that any toy your pet likes well enough to play with will end up in its mouth, you need to screen proposed playthings pretty carefully. Whether homemade or store-bought, the toy should be sturdy enough to take a fair amount

Below: *The red mite is a parasite that feeds at night by sucking blood from its host.*

of chewing, safe enough to prevent poisoning or injury, and cheap enough so that you can replace it periodically without breaking the bank.

Some very nice, not terribly costly toys should be available in the pet store or pet-supply house. Wooden swings are such a universal favorite among cockatiels (and, indeed, any parrot) that this item should almost certainly be on your list. Sturdy rawhide-chew donuts or lava-rock-and-hardwood combinations are especially tough and long-lasting, but metal mirrors and bells are also strong enough to take the cockatiel's attentions. You may have to experiment a bit. All cockatiels are individuals, and you can't predict which toy is going to catch its fancy. I have a young hen who determinedly destroyed a chain-suspended lava rock meant to keep a macaw busy; she eagerly set aside a part of each afternoon to whittle it down. Yet the previous owner of this toy, a sassy conure with a bigger beak, hadn't even touched it, and certainly many other cockatiels would prefer a toy more their own size. You just never know.

One warning: The bright and shiny plastic toys are for budgies, not cockatiels. A cockatiel might take longer than most parrots to tear a plastic penguin apart and choke on its cute little flippers, but it can happen. Better safe than sorry.

Some cheap, if very temporary, toys can be provided on a regular basis when you're playing with your cockatiel. Many love to chew up magazine renewal cards, junk mail, wine corks, corrugated packages, toilet paper and towel rolls, and old-fashioned wooden clothespins that lack the wire springs that could trap a cockatiel's foot. All are fine, as long as the paper and cardboard items given are free of colored dyes. The only problem is that parrots often seem to prefer chewing up pretty, colorful things! Soaking a temporary toy in juice or Kool-Aid to soak up a little flavor and color can help make up for the fact that you refuse to let your pet chew up that shocking pink postcard.

The very best toy any cockatiel can have is a portable parrot playpen. It doesn't have to be expensive or store-bought, as long as it's light enough for you to carry easily from room to room yet entertaining enough to give your cockatiel plenty to do. A simple plywood tray that can be lined with paper or litter makes an excellent base. A sturdy Y-shaped hardwood branch or a miniature jungle gym of swings and ladders are both excellent. Other hanging toys can be added as inspiration strikes or old components wear out. You don't have to get too fancy; in fact, it's better if you don't. You don't want the cockatiel getting bonked in the head every time it turns around!

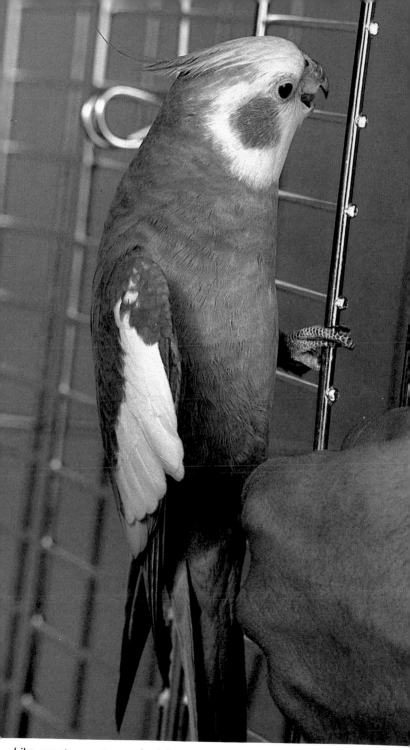

Like most parrots, cockatiels use their beaks to help them climb.

I really can't overemphasize the value of a playpen. A cockatiel at liberty in a room usually likes to go to two or three favorite perches, and a playpen is a much better "home away from home" than an awkward spot on top of the drapes! The fact that you can conveniently enjoy your pet out of its cage even when your hands are busy will encourage you to take it out to play more often, and that's

Above: NYLABIRD *products offer durability, nutrition, exercise, and occupation to a pet cockatiel.*

all to the benefit of the cockatiel's psychological and physical well being.

Cleaning the Cage
For health as well as aesthetic reasons, you need to keep any bird's cage and

Overall, the normal cockatiel hen is colored more dully than the male.

accessories as clean as possible. Theoretically, a single pet bird is far less likely to become exposed to disease organisms than a bird who comes in contact with many others, but you lose that advantage fast if conditions permit harmful bacteria to take root and thrive. Open food and water dishes should be cleaned daily, and while closed seed and water feeders can go for a few days, *any* soft food must be

Below: *In addition to desirable horizontal wiring, this cage features a door that becomes a playground when opened.*

removed after 24 hours. For those days when dishwashing is just too much of a chore, it's nice to have extra interchangeable dishes on hand. Paper-lined tray bottoms should also be changed every day, while litter tray bottoms can be changed every two or three days.

Ideally, you should clean the entire cage once a week. It really isn't as hard as it sounds when you only have the one pet or pair. Pet stores sell small, stiff-wired perch scrapers that make removing caked-on feces from wooden surfaces a breeze. The rest of the cage can be wiped out or hosed down while the cockatiel's visiting another

family member's shoulder or its convenient playpen.

In warm weather, you may take bird, cage, and all outside for a shower. Make sure only a light mist hits the bird, and it will probably love it. Many cockatiels act as if a shower is the height of sensual pleasure, closing their eyes beatifically and stretching wings and head to catch the droplets. You'd swear you could practically hear them purr, and you will definitely hear the indignant squeals if you end the fun too soon! Dry cage and bird off in a half-shaded spot so that your pet can move out of the shade if it gets too warm. Although a desert bird, a cockatiel doesn't like to fry any more than you do. Remember, a hot bird in the wild is free to move into the shade, and your pet cockatiel should be too. If you think it's too cool in the shade, it's probably too cool for a shower. And do give the shower early enough in the day that the bird will have time to dry out before evening.

A warning to owners of red-eyed cockatiels such as lutinos: The black pigment absent from these birds' eyes is what normally protects cockatiels from the intense glare of the sun. Like Hollywood's gremlins, these varieties must be protected from bright light. You may want to keep them indoors, especially if they show any signs of discomfort.

Above: *Pet cockatiels taken outdoors should not be left unsupervised, even if apparently safe in their cages.*

There are some circumstances under which you won't be able to adhere to a strict once-a-week schedule. For instance, if a pair is trying to go to nest, you have no business moving the cage about and upsetting their routine. Don't worry. Good habits in the past will carry you through until you can give a thorough cleaning once more. Of course, you are never excused from providing spotless dishes!

Care and Feeding of the Cockatiel

"Diet" and "nutrition" are words surrounded by more mystery and mystification than any other element of bird care. Almost everyone has heard that birds instinctively know what to eat to meet all their nutritional needs, and almost everyone has heard wrong. Birds are not tiny computers with a running total of minimum daily requirements ticking off in their heads. Instead, like humans and most other omnivores (a word that literally means "eaters of everything"), they tend to eat many different kinds of food, depending on what's available at the moment and what tastes good. If they eat a wide enough variety in sufficient quantity, they'll probably take

Above: *In the wild, cockatiels feed mostly on seeds found on the ground.*

in all the nutrients they need to thrive and reproduce.

The variety of food eaten by wild omnivorous birds is truly staggering. Stomach analyses of various species have shown that literally hundreds of different foods are taken, including various kinds of animal matter such as insects, spiders, and worms, as well as vegetable feed ranging from buds through petals to fruits, seeds, and nuts.

Although cockatiels follow roughly the same pattern, feeding on seeding grasses and incidentally ingesting some protein-rich insects

A well-nourished cockatiel, like this pied, displays sleek, shiny plumage.

along with it, they're better equipped to handle deficiencies than the parrots who didn't evolve to cope with a rugged semi-arid environment. The fact is no doubt a key reason why cockatiels and their Australian buddies the budgies were the first parrots to breed reliably in captivity. Nevertheless, they will certainly live longer and better if provided with an optimum diet instead of a minimal one.

An additional reason for being extra concerned with a captive cockatiel's diet is that there is just no way a house pet can eat the same volume of food as a wild bird. Wild cockatiels, remember, migrate hundreds of miles in search of water, in the process burning far more food energy than any bird hopping around its playpen. Clearly, since the pet can't take in as much food, what food it does eat must be especially high in nutrients. For this reason, I think it's useful for the owner of even such a hardy bird as the cockatiel to know a bit about the nutritional basics.

Below: A mixture containing several kinds of seeds is the basis of the diet of a pet cockatiel; yet without supplementation, over time a seed mixture proves nutritionally deficient.

Water

Who would have thought that decent water would be so hard to find? My local water supply is from the Mississippi River, so that we never really know what odd color or strange flavor will come out of the tap next. Since chemical spills have become a way of life, I don't even fill my goldfish tank with tap water, much less permit my birds to drink the stuff! Unless you're quite sure of your water supply, you should stick to tested, bottled waters. In the past, pure distilled water was disparaged because it lacks the calcium and other beneficial minerals that give the best water its pleasant taste. I agree that an uncontaminated natural water is better than distilled, but if you have no other choice, give the distilled stuff and let the bird get its minerals somewhere else.

Cups for food and water are best kept off the floor. Instead, attach them to the cage wires where they can be reached from the perches.

The Basic Diet

In some areas, you can probably get away with boiling tap water to remove the chlorine and any possible bacterial pests. However, you should be aware that boiling doesn't remove many dangerous chemicals. Only you can make the best judgement about what to do in your area.

from sickness and injury. Because there is relatively little protein in seeding grasses, some people think that cockatiels do not need it. That's absolutely untrue. Your pet may get by with less of it than many another bird, but it will die if deprived indefinitely. Remember, wild cockatiels get protein from the insects

The Basic Diet

There are three main kinds of food—protein, fat, and carbohydrate. All foods are made of these basic ingredients, and for optimum health, your cockatiel should get a balanced supply of each. But what exactly are these components, and how do you get them into your bird?

Protein is the building block of life. It is used whenever the body grows or repairs itself. There is no substitute for protein. A baby chick will cease to grow and will die without it, and an adult bird will have difficulty recovering

Above: *Most cockatiels enjoy greens.*

they swallow along with their seeds, but since your home is hopefully bugfree, you'll have to supply your pet with another protein source.

Carbohydrates and fats, the main components of seeds and grains, are the energy foods. Carbohydrates (sugars and starches) are readily digested for use by the body as fuel for moment-to-moment activities. Fat is more compact and complex, providing a source of energy that can be stored by the body for times when less food is available. Since you won't be starving your pet, fat is the least crucial element of the diet. As with people, it's better to store food in the larder than around the waist! Nevertheless, some amount of fat should always be left in the diet to provide the oils needed for healthy feathers.

It's worth noting that if, for some odd reason, a bird eats nothing but protein, its body can break down some of that food for energy. But in the more usual case where a bird eats only the energy-givers, its body can't build a protein from the carbohydrates and fats. To sum up, all three elements are necessary, but protein is absolutely irreplaceable.

Besides the big three, birds also need the minuscule components found in food, namely, vitamins and minerals. Vitamins are complex chemicals that help the body use food efficiently to maintain health and construct new tissues while minerals are simple elements used to complete the building of healthy bones, blood, and other structures. A deficiency of even one key vitamin or mineral can lead to disease or even death of the bird. However, since a bird's body makes its own vitamin C as well as some of the B vitamins, the most common deficiencies seen in cage birds are lack of vitamins A and D and the mineral calcium. Since all three work together in preparing the female for egg-laying, these

deficiencies are particularly dangerous to hens. Don't suppose that your pet is safe because she's unmated. The proof that unmated birds can lay eggs is no further than your own refrigerator; all of those chicken eggs sold in grocery stores are unfertilized by a male unless the box specifically tells you otherwise.

Well, so much for theory. Now how do we go about getting all these nutritional goodies into our pet bird? There are several good approaches, but ultimately, the choices you make will depend upon how much time and money you can spend on

Below: *Today commercial seed mixtures often contain, in addition to seeds, dietary supplements designed to make the mixture a better balanced diet.*

feed, and what your particular cockatiel will actually eat.

Many people still give their cockatiels a simple seed cup supplemented only with greens, the occasional bit of apple, and a mineral block. From what I said earlier, you

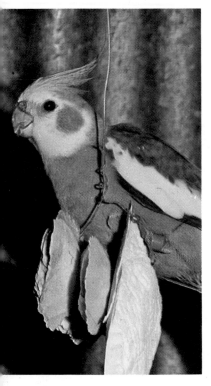

Above: *Cuttlebones or mineral blocks are the usual ways to ensure adequate amounts of minerals— notably calcium—in the diet.*

can probably figure out that their pets are short on protein. Since cockatiels are tough birds, healthy nonbreeding adults can do well for a long time on such a diet. But should they get sick or injured, their bodies can't

repair themselves efficiently, putting them at much higher risk for their lives. The situation is particularly hazardous for a laying female, since her body will steal nutrient supplies from her bones and other vital organs to form the egg. Let's look at some simple ways to add protein to the diet so that you won't have to risk a beloved pet's life.

The easiest method is to offer one of the new pelleted cockatiel formulations as the basis of your pet's diet. A lot of time and effort has gone into making these new feeds the most balanced cage-bird diets ever. Although by far the costliest option, they're certainly worthwhile when convenience is more important than price. A cheaper and more traditional method is to combine a good seed mix with a good protein food such as game-bird starter, mynah pellets, or dog food. The problem here is that many cockatiels will pick out all the seeds and leave the protein food behind, effectively proving that they'd rather eat what they like than what's good for them! (Most cockatiels won't touch dry dog food with a ten-foot pole.) I've found it better to offer seed and game-bird starter or mynah pellets on alternate days. The protein dish may be greeted with a squeal of rage, but at least it gets eaten! Some people prefer to offer the protein food in the morning and the seed bowl in the afternoon. Whatever works for you is fine. Remember that vitamin powder sprinkled on seeds may get thrown away with the shell, but vitamin powder on the protein foods will get where you want it to go.

If you're prepared to do a little cooking, you can whip up a better-liked alternative in the kitchen. Eggs are the highest quality protein known, and they're also a good source of vitamins. A hard-boiled, mashed egg should be greeted with the utmost enthusiasm. If you mix the egg with a teaspoon each of powdered avian vitamins and a milkfree protein powder for people, the egg mash will be

Below: *That water should be changed daily is an important point of hygiene in keeping cockatiels.*

dry enough to sit out 24 hours. Otherwise, it's best to remove the dish after an hour.

To round out the diet, green food and a mineral block or cuttlebone should be available on a daily basis. Well-chosen green food is a good vitamin source, while the mineral block provides much-needed calcium for healthy bones and eggs. Vegetable sprouts, kale, spinach, dandelions, and dark green lettuce are best. Iceberg lettuce, the pale kind used in most American salads, is unfortunately almost totally devoid of vitamins or flavor, so you should switch to darker greens for your own sake as well as your pet's. Give a fresh supply each day. Mineral blocks and cuttlebones, found in pet stores, can be hung in the cockatiel's cage until eaten or soiled.

The Cockatiel at Dinner

The grit cup is a puzzling element of a pet cockatiel's diet for some people. "Why should I feed my bird crushed rocks?" they wonder. The answer's simple: Birds lack

Below: *Some cages are designed so that food cups may be serviced from the outside.*

teeth, so they swallow bits of stone to grind up food particles in their stomachs. A little goes a long way, and one box is more than your cockatiel will eat in its whole lifetime! Because a stressed or nervous bird may eat an excessive amount of grit, always remove the grit cup during periods of stress such

as illness, injury, a change of home or environment, or introduction to another bird.

The Cockatiel at Dinner

Many pet cockatiels love nothing better than sharing your dinner. Because cockatiels, like humans, are omnivores, giving people food to your bird can be very beneficial if you're wise about what you eat. It can also be an unqualified disaster! Here are a few tips to make mealtimes healthy as well as fun.

Soft drinks and other beverages are out. You don't want your cockatiel to get in the habit of sticking its head way down in the bottom of a glass to slurp some sweet fluid. Too many pets have drowned that way when their owner was out of the room. Milk is sometimes suggested as a health beverage for birds, but actually it's quite worthless to them since their bodies lack the ability to digest it. (After all, milk is one of the things that make us mammals different from birds; the very word *mammal* derives from the presence of the milk-producing mammary glands in mammalian mothers.)

Salads, on the other hand, are great if you don't waste your time with limp canned fruit and pallid iceberg lettuce. Small bits of fresh vegetables and fruits are excellent treats. Unless the veggies are daubed with a bit of dressing, the fruits will

Apart from hulling seeds, a cockatiel's beak is designed to tear large pieces of food into smaller ones.

probably be better liked, but both are valuable and easy to offer in small chunks. Many people give their parrots their own miniature salad bowl, a great way to keep your cockatiel's head out of *your* plate.

Whether or not you should offer treats from the main course depends on how well you yourself eat. In general, you should avoid filling up your pet on non-nutritious foods that will crowd protein, vitamins, and minerals out of

eat are bits of fruit, cheese, seed, and nuts. (Although a dairy product, the processing of cheese naturally converts it into a more digestible form than the milk from which it came.) No sugar! No candy, ice cream, cake, or cookies! I promise you that you'll be sorry if you break this rule even once. Sugar is a wonderful perverter of taste buds, and the average cockatiel has no more self-control around it than the average human. Unless you

its diet. The more natural, unrefined foods such as whole-wheat bread, whole-grain pastas and cereals, and brown rice are excellent; white bread, ordinary pasta, and white rice are not. Lightly cooked vegetables, perhaps with a small amount of butter or cheese, are probably best. Be stingy with meat. It's high in fat as well as protein, and if you give your cockatiel any seed at all, it already has enough fat.

The only desserts and snacks your cockatiel should

Above: *Pet cockatiels often want to try the foods their owners enjoy.*

want the rest of your desserts for the next ten years to be accompanied by peremptory squeals for a nibble, avoid giving your pet the chance to develop a sweet beak.

Handling the Picky Eater
The wild cockatiel isn't a picky eater. It couldn't afford to be, not in its harsh environment. The domesticated cockatiel

Sprays of millet are nutritious, and cockatiels enjoy nibbling the small seeds from the stalk.

can be a bird of quite a different feather. While you can make sure that birds you've raised yourself develop the best nutritional habits, an older bird comes with a set of likes and dislikes that can be quite resistant to change. I have a female cockatiel so set in her ways that although she's tame enough to beg me to scratch her ears, she absolutely won't take treats from the hand. Or from the dish. Or from any other place

pouting. But for the sake of your pet's health, it's worth it. Remove the seeds and leave only the most nutritious foods. At your meals, offer vegetable bits lightly coated with dressing or ripe bits of fruit. Sometimes it helps if the cockatiel sees *you* eating the food in question; some pets will only eat lettuce, for instance, when they can grab it from your salad plate. While the seed's out of the diet, you can be a little freer about

I've been able to think of. Left to her own devices, she carefully picks out the tiny millet seeds—chosen, no doubt, because they're the least nutritious stuff in the bowl—and completely ignores everything else.

To get something other than a favorite seed into a picky eater, you may have to put up with a few angry squeals and some eloquent

Commercially available cockatiel treats are designed to be both nutritious and appealing.

offering high-calorie treats from your plate, which should console the cockatiel and convince it that other foods can taste good too.

Above: *Offering food in the hand will promote a cockatiel's tameness.*

Below: *After bathing, birds spend considerable time preening to rearrange their plumage.*

The Well Groomed Cockatiel

A good diet will go a long way toward producing a beautiful cockatiel, but for perfect plumage, you need to know a bit about keeping your pet well groomed. I already talked about bathing in the previous chapter, but let me comment here that most cockatiels prefer a spray bath to splashing in an open tub of water. In hot weather (and any time if a family member is allergic), spray at least once a day. If you forget, you may get splashed by a furious bird forcing itself into its water dish! Always spray gently in a warm location, with plenty of time for cockatiel and cage to dry before bedtime.

People differ on the issue of clipping a cockatiel's wings. These birds are more flight-oriented than most parrots, so that they may not get

Above: *Some cockatiels are not inclined to bathe in a dish of water.*

Below: *One style of feather trimming allows two or three feathers to remain uncut at the end of the wing to preserve a good appearance.*

enough exercise if they can't fly. On the other hand, many a flighted cockatiel has flown out the door, become confused, and been lost forever. If you tend to be absent-minded about leaving doors open or walking outdoors with a bird on your shoulder, you'll probably want to keep your pet's wings clipped. If a new cockatiel isn't tame, ask the seller to clip its wings for you to make the taming process easier.

It's easy to clip a cockatiel's wings, once you've seen how it's done, and it isn't any more painful to the bird than it is for you to have your hair cut. Have a helper hold the cockatiel gently while you stretch out one wing. Clip only the long outer feathers on the lower end of the wing to prevent hitting a still-growing "blood feather." Clipping three or four feathers on one side won't completely stop flight, but it will prevent the cockatiel from getting much lift or control over the direction it's flying, discouraging wild escapes, if not short hops about the room.

Oftentimes, a cockatiel that spends a lot of time in a cage develops overgrown claws and beak. An overgrown beak is a serious problem that can actually prevent the bird from eating enough to stay healthy. Since it's easily prevented by giving challenging chew toys like lava rocks and rawhide doughnuts, your pet shouldn't have this problem. But if it does, you should probably let a vet or a professional pet groomer handle the tricky job of trimming back the beak.

Claw-clipping is much easier—a lucky thing, since overgrown nails are much more common. You'll need some supplies: an old towel, a nail file, a pair of dog clippers, and some styptic powder. Have a helper hold the cockatiel gently in the towel, being careful not to press on its chest or diaphragm.

Quickly clip or file the very end of the bird's nails. It's better to take too little and have to repeat the job next week than to clip too much

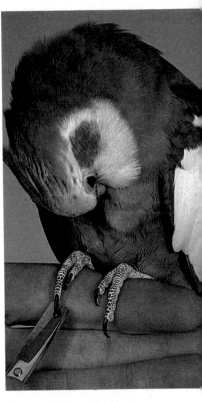

Above: *Scissors with notched blades facilitate claw clipping, as does the bird's tameness.*

and draw blood. If you do have an accident, though, quickly press a bit of styptic powder against the end of the claw. The bleeding should stop quickly. In pale-footed varieties of cockatiels, it will be easy to avoid the vein since you'll be able to see where it runs through the claw.

57

Taming and Training

Taming a young cockatiel is easy, especially if you've chosen a bird under two or three months old. (Remember to check for a pink beak!) Experts differ in their favorite techniques, but all methods boil down to two types— gradual or intensive. The gradual method is best for very wild birds such as older cockatiels because it allows the bird to get used to human company without putting too great a stress on its system.

Above: *A finger pressed against the cockatiel's breast induces him to step up.*

Youngsters just out of the nest can handle more intensive training because their young minds and bodies aren't yet set into wild habits. Such adaptable specimens can be scampering about on your arm within minutes of

Adult cockatiels, whether male or female, are less amenable to training than young birds.

beginning the first training session.

Because an early start is so important to easy taming, you don't have a moment to lose once you get the new pet home. However, don't hover over its cage for the first few days or hours; it needs time to get used to the new situation and to relax enough to eat and drink. In the unlikely event that it doesn't settle down enough to eat after 24 hours, you should contact the seller for help. Otherwise, you're ready to begin.

It's absolutely essential that you tame the bird in a quiet, isolated spot. Your new pet is overwhelmed enough by the unfamiliar environment. You can't expect it to calm down if other people or birds are standing around watching and offering advice. In fact, until the cockatiel's tame, it should be completely isolated from other birds, and only one person should be allowed to work with it. Even a toy mirror can present a distraction that causes the cockatiel to focus on its reflection instead of its lessons, so consider yourself warned.

Once you're in a quiet, uncluttered room, you can choose the taming method that seems most appropriate to your situation.

Intensive Training: The Young Cockatiel

Intensive training involves subjecting the bird to continuous contact that it can't escape. After a time, the cockatiel's nervous system becomes overwhelmed by your constant attention and the bird stops trying to flee. In a relatively short period, it realizes that being around you is pleasant, not dangerous. Although some experts disagree, I feel obliged to state my opinion that such intensive training is best reserved for very young birds in top-notch condition. Cockatiels rarely die of fright as do some smaller birds, but too much stress always has the potential to allow disease organisms to gain a foothold in the body.

Taming a young cockatiel is quite different from taming larger, wilder birds. You don't need a stick or heavy pair of gloves; although the cockatiel may hiss and threaten, it probably won't bite. The risk of a baby's nibble is certainly worth taking to train the bird to step directly on your hand.

You may start the taming process while the cockatiel is still in its cage. (Again, this technique is quite different from that used with the larger parrots, which bitterly resent any intrusion into their private homes.) I like to start by offering a special treat such as a bit of grape or a twig of millet spray. Slowly, speaking in a soft, reassuring voice all the while, put your hand into the cage with the treat between two fingers. Try to approach from the bird's side, rather than from head-on, which is often interpreted as a

Head study of a female cockatiel.

gesture of aggression. The cockatiel may try to frighten you away by hissing, slashing forward as if to bite, and vigorously flapping its wings. You may pause for a moment, but don't pull back. If you do, you'll have taught the bird that it can scare you away!

Eventually the cockatiel may snatch at the treat in your hands. If it eats it, great. Don't stop praising it in a soft voice. If it merely throws it furiously to the ground, try again. As the cockatiel will almost invariably accept the chance to step up. Don't worry if it uses its beak as a steadying third leg; it won't bite you in the process. Now, with bird on hand, slowly remove your arm from the cage.

Once outside, the cockatiel may panic and try to fly away. If its wings are clipped, it will probably head for the floor; if not, it may make a couple of circuits of the room before landing. In either case, wait

long as you move slowly, without any sudden jerky motions, the cockatiel will soon accept your hand as a normal part of the cage. At that point, it may step on board of its own accord. If not, you can easily encourage it to do so by placing your hand against its chest. Birds instinctively like to perch on the highest spot around, and

Above: *The initial stages of training are designed to accustom the cockatiel to having a person close by.*

until it lands before moving slowly and reassuringly to fetch it. Some trainers actually pick the bird up

Intensive Training: The Young Cockatiel

(gently!) and return it to the hand; I perfer to coax it back onto my hand by placing my forefinger at its chest. In either case, speak softly the whole time to gain the cockatiel's confidence. It may fly away several times, but don't lose patience. It will tire before you do. Once it does decide to remain on your hand, praise it effusively and offer it a special treat.

Now you may try a couple of variations. Using a game called the ladder, you can coax the cockatiel to practice stepping from one hand to the other. While it stands on one hand, place the other level with its chest. When it climbs onto the new hand, place the old one at the new chest level, and so on until you're holding the bird as high as you can in the air. To teach it to leave your hand for its cage, hold it so that the top of the cage is at the level of its chest and it should step off onto the roof. To return it to the cage at the end of the lesson, put hand and bird *slowly* into the cage, holding your hand so that the perch is at the level of the bird's chest. Why all this practice for getting the bird *off* your hand? Well, hard as it may be to believe in the beginning, many pet birds are much harder to get off a beloved arm or shoulder than on!

Once the cockatiel willingly steps on and off your hand on command and is no longer afraid of human company, it is technically tame. You may very well tame your baby in one lesson! However, I do advise taking the time to complete the taming process by teaching it to accept being held and cuddled. Not only does being scratched and petted help keep a pet's feathers in good condition, its being able to tolerate free handling without fear makes claw clipping and vet exams much easier on both of you.

Although some people switch the order, I prefer to start by scratching the cockatiel's cheek patches. Approach its head slowly,

Below: *Since flight is a cockatiel's principal method of escape, wing trimming may significantly facilitate taming.*

The Gradual Method:

from the side, always murmuring reassurances. Don't be discouraged by small feints and hisses. Once you've started to scratch, the cockatiel will calm down amazingly. It will soon learn to beg for the favor by bowing its head and closing its eyes. At that point, you may get hissed or squealed at if you fail to provide the scratching!

Once head-scratching is accepted, work back to patting the cockatiel's back. Gently! It may never learn to actually enjoy this behavior, but it's important that it accept it. Once it resigns itself to back-patting, you should try to slowly and carefully encircle its body with your hand, always keeping the head free and never pressing it on the chest. Put a slight pressure on the wings to prevent it from flapping wildly and hurting itself. Many cockatiels won't like the treatment, but letting them get used to it can make all the difference in the world if it ever has to be handled while sick or injured.

The Gradual Method: For Older or Stressed Cockatiels

If your cockatiel has reached late adolescence or early adulthood without being tamed, you will have to take a little more time with its education. An aviary bird raised by its parents can be surprisingly shy of humans if they weren't part of its day-to-day experience when young. Taming these birds isn't hard, just a matter of time and patience.

You start as before, giving the cockatiel a few hours or overnight to settle into its new home and get something to eat. Then you may start regularly approaching the cage, murmuring reassurances whenever you come by. Don't forget to talk to the bird when you're changing its tray or food!

Below: *Mirrors are appealing because the reflection is taken to be another cockatiel.*

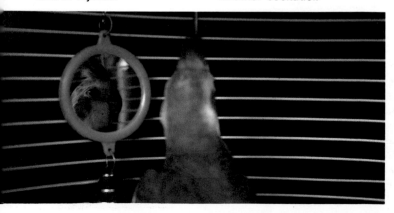

Above: *Most likely, head scratching resembles being preened by a conspecific.*

Take every opportunity to show it that it's safe when you're around. At first it may hiss and protest whenever you approach, but it will soon stop when it sees that threats make no difference in your behavior. Depending on the bird, a few hours or a few days may pass before it's perfectly calm in your presence.

As with the previous method, you must now clear the room of clutter and human as well as avian distractions. Then you may *slowly* put your hand in the cage, again approaching from the bird's side with a small treat between your fingers. If you're especially afraid of being bitten or if the bird in question seems especially

aggressive, you can wear a pair of heavy gloves. However, be aware that you will later have the extra step of training the bird to accept your hand without the gloves. It's really best to offer the bare hand if you can. Keep in mind that although adult cockatiels may inflict pain, they probably won't unless startled. In any case, they're unable to do any real damage. Just move very slowly, stopping but not retreating when your bird acts nervous or aggressive, and you'll both do just fine. In a first session with an older bird, you've achieved your goal when it takes the treat from your fingers or steps onto your hand. Let it rest for an hour or so before repeating the lesson.

You may repeat the lesson several times a day each day, but try not to work longer than 20 or 30 minutes each time. Remember that an older bird needs time to recover from

the taming stress. How long will it take to get an older cockatiel to hop reliably on and off of your hand? I can't give an exact timetable, because so much depends on your patience and the individual personality of your cockatiel. But I would certainly expect even the wildest specimen to step reliably onto your hand within its cage by the end of a week of regular lessons.

Follow the directions given previously for removing the bird from its cage and teaching it to ride about on your finger or shoulder, with the difference that you must accept a much slower rate of progress than with the younger bird. While baby's lesson two may find you scratching its head and patting its back, the adult's doing well if it stays on your hand without immediately flying down. Again, it's better to have several short sessions throughout the course of the day than a single, long, intense one. There's really no

Above: *Since birds do not naturally take to being petted, it must be done very gently.*

need to rush things. Even if it takes as long as a month to train the adult to accept your petting and cuddling—and it probably won't—you've still invested a short amount of taming time in relation to the decade or two of pleasure you can expect from your new pet's company.

Biting

Suppose your cockatiel bites you or starts chewing on something dangerous. What do you do? If the bite is really a harmless nibble, ignoring it will probably tell your pet that biting doesn't work. But if the bite is really painful or you want it to drop something really fast, you should say, "No!" in a loud, firm voice. The unexpected scolding is usually enough to startle the cockatiel loose. If it bites again, repeat the firm "No!"

66

Punishing the cockatiel (or any other bird) will *not* work because it frightens rather than educates the bird. The best way to discourage biting is to encourage your pet's love so that it won't wish to displease you. Fortunately, since cockatiels are so eager for affection, real biting (as opposed to harmless mouthings) is unlikely to persist.

It's unwise to return your cockatiel to its cage immediately after it bites you because you may thus unintentionally teach it that biting is the way to let you know it wants to go back in.

Training

Once the cockatiel's tamed, you'll probably want to train your pet to do tricks or to talk. A wonderful idea! It's a misconception that training is cruel and unnatural. In the wild, a cockatiel spends a lot of time searching for food and water, and avoiding predators. In captivity, where the necessities of life are given, trick training is an excellent way to exercise intellectual capabilities that could otherwise atrophy.

Most home trick training is accomplished by offering food

Below: *While a cockatiel's bite can be painful, its beak is not powerful enough to do serious injury.*

Above: *Untame cockatiels typically retreat to the farthest corner of the cage when approached.*

create an avian ham, you'll be the envy of everyone you know. The only thing cuter than a bird that does tricks is a bird that begs for the chance to do tricks!

Tricks are taught by conditioning the bird to react in the same, desired way each time a particular command is given. For instance, it's valuable to teach a bird to "come." During the first few lessons, the cockatiel may be placed on top of its cage before the command is given. If sufficiently tame, it may fly to your shoulder simply because it wants to be with you, not because you've asked it to come. Nevertheless, you reward it with a treat. After it has responded well to several repetitions, you may place it on another surface, perhaps a table top, and command it to come from there. Be patient, repeating the command if it doesn't fly to you at once. When it finally does get the idea (or just decides to flap on over), heap on the praise and offer the reward. Of course, be prepared for several lessons of no longer than twenty minutes each before the cockatiel learns to respond to the word "come" by automatically heading for you. Be patient. Long, boring lessons or grumpy, irritable ones won't teach your cockatiel that it's fun to obey you!

If you have the odd cockatiel like the hen I mentioned who hates

rewards. Before training begins, you need to observe your cockatiel to see what foods it particularly enjoys. It's also helpful if you cut rations in half, which will make the bird more interested in receiving the food reward. In a tame bird, the desire to please is also a powerful motivation, so don't forget to praise your pet effusively when it does well. There's no such thing as too much praise going to its head. If you do

Above: *This tame young cockatiel stays placidly on the finger as it is returned to its cage.*

everything edible except itty bitty millet seeds, you can offer an affection reward instead of food. In her case, a head-scratching usually gets her purring with delight. The only problem with offering affection rewards is that they do take more time and tend to slow training progress. But, after all, what's the big hurry if you're both having a good time getting there?

To come and to defecate on command are especially useful tricks. Most cockatiels aren't housebroken, but it's certainly possible to teach a smart student to defecate over its cage when you give the word. In order for potty-training to take, you should choose a word not normally used in conversation as the command for defecation. (Otherwise, you could accidentally give the word while you're talking to someone else and have the bird use your new shirt!) You must also be aware that parrots aren't built to "hold it," and cockatiels are no exception. Never expect it to sit on your arm or shoulder for more than 20 minutes without a quick trip to its cage to defecate. Don't punish accidents, and praise the bird highly whenever it goes on command even if you suspect that its performance was just coincidence. It takes longer to potty train a cockatiel than to teach it to perch on your arm or to come on command, but it's worthwhile if you're

Above: *A playground offers exercise opportunities and a change of scene from the cage.*

squeamish or own lots of expensive clothes.

By offering love, patience, and a well-chosen snack, you can also teach a cockatiel a few showier tricks. Because they aren't used to holding food in their claws, they aren't the naturals at pulling or hauling toys that most other parrots are. However, they can do very well at tricks that allow them to use their beaks as hands. Picking up a penny and placing it in a piggy bank is a good example of a fairly complex trick. In the first few lessons, you should reward the bird just for finding and picking up the penny. (It will eventually, if only because the coin is pretty and parrots love bright things.) Next, praise it for taking a few steps with the coin. Later, praise it only when it steps in the direction of the bank. When it approaches the bank, you can tap your fingers near the slot to draw its attention. When at last it drops the penny in the slot, reward it well and praise it highly! In succeeding lessons, you must offer praise only when the bird equals or exceeds previous progress. Once it has learned to put the penny in the slot, for instance, coax it to complete the entire trick before offering a food reward.

Teaching a Cockatiel to Talk

Don't make your love contingent on your cockatiel talking. Most don't talk at all, and few talk as volubly as several other parrot species. In a survey done by *Bird Talk* magazine only one out of 52 cockatiels had a vocabulary of over 100 words. By contrast, 2 out of 6 ringneck parakeets had a vocabulary of over 100 words, and the average number of words spoken by these birds was 77. (The average *talking* cockatiel knew 19 words.) Two 10 or 15 minute sessions morning and night will probably teach your cockatiel to talk if you stick with it, but the first word may not be spoken for several months. Patience and consistency are the watchwords. It's possible for a sharp cockatiel to pick up words in day-to-day conversation, but without some work on your part, it's pretty unlikely.

During speech training, you can hold the cockatiel on your hand or leave it in the cage. If left in the cage, you should remove the feed cup and the toys for the duration of the lesson. Turn off any radios or televisions, and retire to a quiet room free of distractions. Choose a simple word like "Hello" or the bird's name to start with. (Some experts feel that birds learn faster from people with

Below: *The tricks that a bird does best depend on its natural propensities, such as climbing.*

Teaching a Cockatiel to Talk

higher-pitched voices, such as women, girls, and pre-adolescent boys. If several family members are competing for the job, you

Below: *Teaching a cockatiel to talk is best carried out in an environment free of distractions.*

may want to keep this suggestion in mind.) Try not to feel idiotic if the cockatiel just sits and looks at you through the course of several lessons.

If your patience isn't up to repeating one word over and over for 20 minutes a day for

weeks on end, you may want to try playing one of the commercial tapes or records available for training birds. As I write, one enterprising company is even offering a video that you can play on your TV, showing an actual parrot repeating the lesson of the day. If you don't watch so much TV that your cockatiel tunes it out, this option may just do the trick. Otherwise, you can try playing the record each morning before uncovering the bird and each evening after covering it for sleep. In the darkness, it should theoretically have nothing to concentrate on but learning its lesson.

Warning: I once trained a parrot using a tape I played each morning while I took my shower to drown out the repititious sound. Unfortunately, the brat associated the words with background shower noises and tried to speak only when the water was running, meat was sizzling on the stove, the vacuum cleaner was going, or my friends were speaking. Rather than deal with the resulting squawkfest, I eventually abandoned the lessons altogether! The moral of the story is to train your bird to talk when everything else is quiet.

Some birds will only talk around the trainer or trusted members of the family. That's embarrassing after you've already bragged to all the guys at the office about your brilliant bird, but unfortunately

Above: *A cockatiel that is very tame toward its owner may behave very differently toward strangers.*

it isn't at all uncommon. Talking is done to please and draw attention, and a shy bird understandably doesn't wish to draw a stranger's attention. If the visitor is willing and responsible, you may allow him or her to hold the cockatiel on hand or shoulder. If you're all gentle rather than boisterous and speak to the bird in low, kind voices, you may elicit a conversation once your pet feels comfortable in the guest's presence. Don't push it. It's when you least expect it that your bird's likely to break in with a pert, "Hello!"

Breeding the Cockatiel

The cockatiel is a naturally prolific bird that's easy to breed if certain requirements are met. However, in most cases, cockatiels usually won't breed as successfully in cages as in pens, and the hobby breeder working with a few cages may encounter more problems per pair than the pen breeder. Experience helps, so don't be discouraged if you have some failures at first. You may not produce birds by the ton, but following the basic rules should ensure you some very nice, healthy chicks.

Cockatiels are sexually mature and able to breed at six months, in many cases before an inexperienced human eye can tell whether the youngster is male or female! Nevertheless, they shouldn't be bred until they're

Above: *Pearl and lutino chicks in a nest box, four to five weeks old, just prior to fledging.*

over a year old, and most experts recommend waiting until the younger member of a pair is at least eighteen months. Very young cockatiels aren't ready to settle down and take on the responsibilities of caring for eggs and babies, and their restlessness can mean broken or abandoned eggs, or negligent or no feeding of hatchlings. Young hens are at special risk for disease or nutritional problems if they breed too young, since the demands of their own growing bodies will compete with the developing egg for vitamins, minerals, and protein. Finally,

With cockatiels, mutual preening serves to reinforce the bond
of mated pairs.

Breeding the Cockatiel

waiting until the birds are older allows you to be sure that you do, in fact, possess a pair.

In many cases, a pet owner just getting interested in breeding will have only one adult cockatiel and will need to acquire a mate for it. To get a bird of the right sex, you need to buy either another adult or a juvenile of known sex. Although it means another wait, buying a younger bird is usually better for beginners because adults on the market are often specimens that have shown breeding problems in the past. (Otherwise, the breeder would have kept them!) But how do you know whether the youngster is a boy or a girl? Usually, of course, you don't, but there is one exception— the product of carefully mated parents chosen so that males will be one color and females the other. In that case, the breeder will be able to tell you what's what and who's who.

To see why this can be done, we must recall that the sex of a baby bird is determined by the genes, chemical messages that come from each parent. The structure that carries a large number of genes is called a chromosome. If a chick is male, it has received an X chromosome (named for its shape) from each parent. If it's female, it has received an X chromosome from its father and a Y chromosome from its mother. The Y chromosome doesn't carry as much

information as the X chromosome. Traits carried on the X but not the Y chromosome are called sex-linked, because their expression is related to the sex of the bird in question. Conveniently, for our purposes, certain color mutations, including the popular lutino, are sex-linked. The upshot of all this hairy theory is that if the father is pure, his daughters will always be the same color that he is since they won't receive conflicting color instructions from their mother, the donor of the incomplete Y chromosome that makes them female. His sons, however, receiving complete X chromosomes, may receive conflicting color instructions from each parent. If mother is a pure gray, the dominant color, while father is lutino, the sons' bodies will exhibit the dominant gray from the two choices carried in their pair of X chromosomes. Therefore, by a careful choice of parents, the offspring may be forced to be all lutino females and gray males, and it will be obvious who's who well before sexual maturity. You must realize that this technique only works if a breeder is careful about keeping records and pairing *pure* birds!

If you can't find sexed youngsters, you should be as choosy as possible about the adult you take home to mate with your bird. Culled show-quality birds may be excellent

In the cockatiel, the factor that produces the lutino coloration
is linked with those that determine sex.

Preparations

parents for the beginner, even if they aren't top prize winners. Moving sales and the like may also be good opportunities to get a bird being sold for no fault of its own.

Although usually sweet-natured, the occasional cockatiel will let you know it wants to reproduce through will breed reliably. If you're housing the potential parents in a cage of less than 2½ feet long and 2 feet tall, you will probably not have much luck unless you allow them to spend a good deal of time with the cage door open, so that they have the option to fly about as the urge takes them. Since it isn't wise to give

an unexpected personality change. Two common symptoms of the urge to mate are nipping and a sudden insistence on being handled by only one family member. Sometimes it will also suddenly decide it only likes humans of one sex.

Preparations
A cockatiel pair needs to feel in control over a certain amount of space before they

Above: *The nest box for this pair is mounted outside the cage.*

cockatiels unsupervised freedom in most households, you will simply have to spring for bigger accommodations if no one is home during the day to keep the loving couple out of trouble. Some breeders have had reliable results with cages 3 feet long, 1½ feet wide, and 2 feet tall. Four feet

Cockatiels of the same sex housed together provide companionship for one another.

long is even better, and the ideal situation is the long flight pen that allows optimum opportunity for exercise.

In the wild, cockatiels nest in holes in rotting or dead trees. Because they had to adapt to a variety of sizes and shapes depending upon what they found in the wild, they learned to be pretty accepting of a wide assortment of nests.

inches wide, and a foot tall, with an entrance hole, 2½ to 3 inches in diameter, some three inches below the top. Place a sturdy perch below the entrance hole. Many people use a hinged roof to simplify checking on the progress of the nest, but since cockatiels are often nervous about being looked down on, you may prefer to

For aviary or cage use, it's better to buy or make a nest box rather than to try to use a found log because the natural nest is harder to clean and may introduce mites into the cage. Cockatiel nest boxes are a standard item at pet stores specializing in birds as well as at pet-supply houses. You may also build them yourself for relatively little effort. Use a hardwood or exterior-grade plywood to prevent the cockatiels from chewing it to bits. The dimensions should run about 10 to 14 inches long, 10

Above: *Nest boxes for cockatiels typically follow this design.*

make a small door in the back instead. In any case, hang the nest as high as you practically can.

What about nesting material? Opinions differ. Wild cockatiels don't usually line their nest hollows, and many breeders don't either, simply chiseling out a small depression on the nest-box bottom to keep the eggs from rolling around. Others prefer

Above: *Housing several cockatiels in the same enclosure allows them to choose mates they prefer.*

to use a layer of pine or cedar shavings. Some have success with peat or sod linings, which are good for very-low-humidity environments such as many temperature-controlled homes, but may allow the growth of harmful molds and bacteria in more humid areas.

A high-quality diet is particularly important at breeding time. The hen, especially, will need protein, calcium, and vitamins to form healthy eggs that are easily passed. She may demolish cuttlebone after cuttlebone with surprising speed to meet her calcium needs, so have extras on hand. Hard-boiled eggs, fresh fruits and vegetables, and other foods will also be taken in larger quantities. The male should also be well-fed, of course,

Care of the Eggs

since caring for the young takes a lot of energy, and he accepts an equal share in incubating the eggs and rearing the brood.

It's much easier to introduce your pet cockatiel to a potential mate than it is to introduce potential partners of most other parrot species. Although the occasional pair may not hit it off, most cockatiels are very good about accepting the mates chosen for them. The

Below: *In the wild, cockatiels nest in tree cavities.*

only problem that may arise is if you break up a pair to mate an inexperienced bird with an experienced breeder. As long as the experienced partner can hear its former mate calling, it will not accept the new bird. Nevertheless, since the benefits of having a more experienced bird coach an inexperienced one are so great, it's worthwhile to take this option while using extreme care to separate former partners aurally as well as visually.

Care of the Eggs

If both parents are beginners, especially if they're "underage," they may neglect or break the eggs, yet care for future broods perfectly. Don't let first-time nerves, either yours or theirs, ruin the breeding experience for you. It's valuable to remember that nature allows for a certain loss of eggs and chicks to accident or disease, and since youngsters are particularly vulnerable, a certain percentage won't survive even under the best conditions. Relax, do your best, and don't blame yourself or the birds if everything doesn't go perfectly at first. Even experienced breeders have losses.

Expect your hen to lay four to seven white eggs at the rate of one every other day. At first the hen may spend a lot of time inside the nest, with the cock sitting just outside on the perch, but once incubation begins, he will also

Above: *At hatching, cockatiels are covered with a sparse yellow down.*

disappear inside the nest box for long periods of time since the male usually broods the eggs during the day. The hen usually takes her turn at night. There are exceptions, and sometimes the birds work out their own schedule. Don't fret too much, but do notice if the cock isn't helping at all, because you will want to limit breeding to prevent exhausting the hen.

It's valuable to offer more spray showers or even a shallow tub of pure water for bathing during incubation, especially when breeding indoors. The cockatiel often returns to the nest box with wet feathers in order to provide the eggs with the moisture they will need to hatch properly.

It's a good idea to check on the progress of the eggs once a day, to get the parents used to your looking in the box. With tame cockatiels, your daily checkups shouldn't frighten them enough to cause them to abandon the eggs. On the sixth day after incubation has begun, you should check the eggs for fertility so that the parents won't have to waste their energy on infertile eggs. An experienced eye can readily distinguish the clear, infertile eggs from the opaque, developing ones by holding them up to a bright light. A beginner, however, should avoid mistakenly tossing good eggs by preparing a simple candler for checking fertility. Enclose a light bulb within a box with a small hole on top for holding the egg. When you look through the egg at the light, you should be able to make out the blood vessels of the developing embryo. If the egg is translucent instead, it is infertile.

Care of the Young

The eggs should begin hatching some time between 17 to 21 days, sometimes taking a while longer if the temperature is low or the brooding irregular. Although downy rather than naked at hatching, the chicks are entirely helpless and blind. Yet, when well-brooded and fed by its parents, a chick may reach half its final body weight by the end of its first week of life! Such rapid growth cannot be sustained without protein, and it's best to offer lots of egg food, crumbles, and other protein-rich foods as well as soaked or sprouted seed. Because the eggs are laid over a period of days and some cockatiels don't wait until all the egg are laid to start brooding, the first-hatched may be much larger than the last-hatched for a while. Fortunately, unlike many bird species in which parents only feed the larger and stronger babies, cockatiels are very good about making sure the runt of the litter gets it share of the food.

At around seven to ten days, the chick becomes the right size to receive a metal band. Soon the foot will grow too big to allow the ring's removal without wire cutters, giving the bird a permanent identification bracelet. This convenient ID helps simplify bloodline records and proves that you bred the bird for show or sale purposes. It may also come in handy if the bird is ever lost or stolen. If you've checked on the brood daily, removing the young for a short period to band them shouldn't cause the parents to refuse to feed them when they're returned to the nest box. Official bands may be obtained from either the American Cockatiel Society or the National Cockatiel Society.

If the parents aren't banded, they may be especially annoyed by the appearance of a bright shiny ring on each of their young.

Below: *A cockatiel pair mating near a tree trunk that is their nest.*

Above: *The smallest chick is three days old, the others more than a week.*

To prevent them from tossing the irritant—and baby with it—you may blacken the ring by holding it over a burning candle. (Be sure it's cool before you try to band the chicks!) It isn't hard to slip the ring over the toes of the baby at this age, but to make it easier, use a tiny dab of petroleum jelly. Many people place the back two toes against the leg and point the front two toes forward before slipping on the ring. Others find it easier to hold the three largest toes forward so that the ring has only to pass over the smallest toe along with the leg. Whatever works for you is fine.

Expect the chicks to fledge—take flight—within four or five weeks of hatching. They aren't quite ready to eat on their own, however. Either you or the parents should keep feeding them for another 2 to 3 weeks. At that point, the parents may want to start another brood. To preserve their health and vitality, remove the nest box after they have produced two or three clutches in a given year. Otherwise, a dedicated pair could breed themselves to exhaustion.

Artificial Incubation and Hand-rearing

First-timers may get flustered and abandon their eggs or a hard-working hen may lay more eggs than she can efficiently raise. What to do? Breeders of several pairs can

Artificial Incubation and Hand-rearing

foster their extras to a pair with an excess of infertile eggs or simply divide up the eggs among several nests, but a beginner isn't likely to have that option. If you have just the one pair, you must either incubate the eggs yourself or toss them in hopes of better luck next time.

Before beginning an incubation project, be aware that cockatiel chicks are fairly fragile and quite demanding during the first two weeks of life. In particular, during the first week, the babies will have to be fed once every 2 or

Below: *When a month old, a cockatiel chick is completely covered with feathers.*

3 hours. If there is no one home during the day to provide regular feedings, you can't take on the job. Don't feel bad if you must toss the eggs. Nature allows for such losses; if every cockatiel produced to its maximum capacity, we would be knee-deep in birds by now!

It may happen that you want to schedule the eggs to hatch during a student's summer vacation or other period that will allow someone to be home to tend the brood. Figure that the eggs will hatch after around 3 weeks in the incubator. To store them until you're ready to start, put them in a cool cupboard or other place where the temperature is between 40° and 60° Fahrenheit. Turn them once or twice a day to keep the embryo from sticking to one side of the shell. It's best if you plan not to store them longer than 2 weeks to a month, because they're much less likely to hatch after prolonged periods of storage.

Storebought incubators can be pricey, so you may wish to build your own. I have used a homemade styrofoam box, designed from junk by a friend, with great success. It's heated by a 40-watt light bulb wired to a relay that switches it on and off at intervals to maintain the proper temperature. Since my talented hobbyist was able to repair a discarded air-conditioning thermostat to regulate the internal temperature, my incubator

The pied mutation inhibits the deposition of melanin pigment when the feathers are formed. Pied cockatiels vary widely in appearance.

Above: *A young cockatiel shows conspicuous barring.*

cost less than a couple of dollars. (Only the light-bulb socket and relay had to be purchased from a store.) However, if you must buy a working thermostat, you'll find that they run at least $20 or $30, making it just as worthwhile to go ahead and buy a cheap incubator kit. Some people do have success using a light bulb alone, without a thermostatic regulator, but the odds are against it.

The simplest incubators will maintain only the temperature, in contrast to expensive versions that rotate the eggs, maintain humidity, and regulate air flow. With the cheaper versions, be sure to turn the eggs yourself twice a day, removing the lid for a bit to let some fresh air into the box. It's also useful to keep a half-filled cup of water in the box to provide moisture. You can also take a tip from the parents and occasionally mist the eggs with water. Don't overdo it, though; too much dampness is as bad as too little. Set the thermostat to 100°F.

It is especially important to candle incubator eggs after a few days of incubation, since infertile eggs left inside an incubator may explode. Believe me, your nose doesn't want that to happen. Besides producing a horrid odor, the molds harbored in rotten eggs can also kill your otherwise healthy embryos or chicks.

If some of the eggs don't hatch on time, you may

The melanin pigments that produce much of a normal cockatiel's markings are absent from the lutino.

wonder whether you should open them and help the chicks out. In my experience, this "help" is rarely a good idea. If it isn't strong enough to make it out of the egg by itself, it probably isn't going to make it anyway—and it's a lot more heart-breaking to lose a chick than an egg.

The first two weeks after hatching are the toughest. If you possibly can, you should leave the youngsters with the parents for this period even if you wish to handfeed for special tameness. But, if you must—and you certainly must

Below: *Cockatiel youngsters in an outdoor flight.*

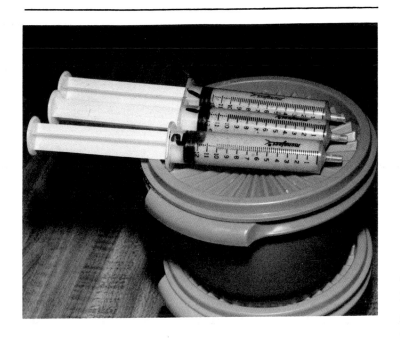

Above: *Syringes filled with a formula in preparation for hand-rearing.*

if the parents didn't even care for the eggs—then you should lower the incubator temperature to 95°F for the first seven days, lower it again to 90° for the next seven days, and so on until you reach room temperature. The chicks will tell you if they're not comfortable; cold chicks will huddle together near the heat source and have trouble digesting their food, while overheated chicks will separate and hold their heads up. It's important to change the lining that the babies sit on often to prevent infection; plastic trays, soft towels, and disposable diapers are popular linings that are easily

replaced for cleaning.

People who don't own incubators or brooders have had excellent results using glass aquariums heated by an infrared lamp or a heating pad. Use a small jar with holes punched in the top to maintain humidity while preventing babies from accidentally drowning themselves in an open cup of water. Whatever you do, you'll need to keep the top partly open to provide fresh air, so use a screen cover if the room isn't secure from curious pets and small children.

Feeding and growing are the big chores during the first few weeks of life. Your handling will ensure that the babies are naturally tame without the need for special lessons. Many, many baby-

Above: *With older chicks, a spoon is often the preferred hand-rearing tool.*

cockatiel formulas have been used with great success, and naturally everyone is fiercely loyal to the mixture that has worked best for him or her. If convenience is important, you can use one of the commercial baby-bird formulas. Although they may be too costly for large breeders, they can be very cost-effective for the small hobbyist who has a lot of leftovers after mixing up a home formula.

If you make your own formula, keep in mind the need for protein! Although most good formulas will be based on some good carbohydrate such as sunflower meal, cornmeal, or oatmeal, there must also be some kind of protein component to permit proper growth. The easiest way to do this is to use a high-protein (human) baby cereal. A simple basic mix could contain 2 cups of the baby cereal; ½ cup cornmeal, powdered oatmeal, or sunflower meal; and ¼ cup powdered wheat germ. (The wheat germ and sunflower meal are found in health-food stores. Notice that good-quality wheat germ and sunflower meal must be stored in the refrigerator, since the vitamin E and related oils can spoil quickly at room temperature.) To use, *slowly* add boiling water to a few heaping spoonfuls, and let it cool until it's lukewarm. Be sure to test the formula against your wrist or lip each time you use it; if it's too cold, baby won't be able to digest it; too hot and it could burn through the crop.

You were wondering just how much water you should add to the formula? Well, that's where experience comes in, even when using a commercial feed. If you are handfeeding from day one, start with a thin gruel that runs easily off a spoon. (The commercial-feed label will suggest using equal amounts of water and feed, but go a little heavier on the liquid at first.) Thicken the consistency of the formula *gradually* over the course of the next two weeks until it resembles canned applesauce. An eye dropper or syringe sturdy enough to be sterilized by boiling between feedings is the easiest way to give the infant formula. Fill the crop, but don't stuff it to the bursting point no matter how loudly the baby pleads!

Below: *Cleaning up after hand-feeding can be done with a moistened cotton swab; otherwise, food may harden and lead to problems.*

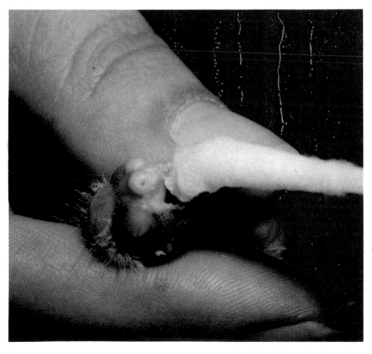

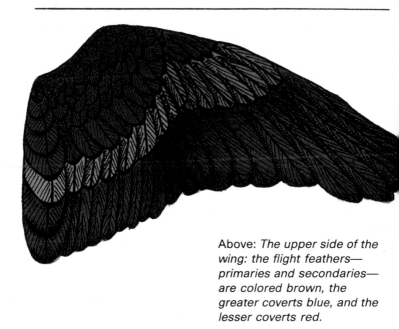

Above: *The upper side of the wing: the flight feathers—primaries and secondaries—are colored brown, the greater coverts blue, and the lesser coverts red.*

However, if you do overfeed, you will soon know it because the crop will still be more than half full when you return for the next feeding. In that case, give only a small amount of pure warm water to give the crop time to empty normally.

For the first 10 days to 2 weeks, feed the hatchlings every 2 to 3 hours between 7 A.M. and 10 P.M. Some people feed round-the-clock, but in most cases, night feeding is really unnecessary since healthy chicks normally go through the night without eating. After 10 days, you can taper down to feeding 6 times a day during the third and fourth week. Actually, it's possible to get away with feeding only 4 times a day during the second two weeks of life, but it's really safer to offer less food per feeding at several feedings. These older chicks may take their thicker formula from a small spoon instead of a syringe. Whether fed with a spoon or a syringe, the little brood can be messy, so be sure to wipe the beak area with a soft towel after each feeding.

At 5 or 6 weeks, the youngsters should be ready to leave the brooder for the cage, but they'll still need supplementary feeding. Put a tube-type water font in the cage and cover the cage floor with a selection of various small seeds to encourage them to investigate the possibility of feeding themselves. (Clean the floor every day, despite the "waste.") Drop a feeding at the beginning of the fifth week and another at the beginning of the sixth. By the seventh week, the chicks should be cracking seed for themselves, but you still need to check on their progress each evening. If a baby's crop is empty at bedtime, feed it a good helping of formula.

Often hand-raised babies take longer to wean than parent-raised birds, and sometimes you'll get an attention-hog which seems as if it might insist on being waited on hand and foot forever. Don't dispair: it too will grow up one day. Don't stop checking its crop each evening and offering it formula if it hasn't eaten, but do encourage it to sample treats during the day by offering millet spray, soaked seed, eggfood, or other goodies. Most of the time, cockatiels learn from each other, so that once you have one chick feeding itself, the rest will quickly follow.

Common Breeding Problems

The upcoming list of problems may make you call me a liar when I report that cockatiels are easy to breed. Relax. Many of the most common problems can be largely prevented through careful attention to proper nutrition and cleanliness. It's a good idea to look over the potential hazards and do a little preventive work to protect your birds and make breeding a joy.

Starting with the (attempted) laying of the egg, egg binding is the first problem we face. Egg binding, a condition where the hen can't pass her egg, is particularly heartbreaking

Below: *The underside of the wing: the primaries and secondaries are shown in brown, while the greater and lesser underwing coverts appear in blue and red, respectively.*

because it threatens the life of your hen as well as her potential brood. Many eggs are hard to pass because they're soft or irregular, probably as the result of a calcium or vitamin deficiency. Remember, even if your hen has all the cuttlebone in the world, her body can't use it unless she also takes in vitamins A and D. Other causes of egg binding are lack of exercise or obesity, both of which may prevent her from moved a good way down the reproductive tract, you may be able to feel it through the abdominal wall. Be gentle! She will most likely die if the egg is broken within her. If a hen is egg bound, you must act at once to save her life. If she's fairly spry, you may be able to help her yourself by holding her in a towel over moist heat to relax the vent. A safe, easy source of moist heat comes from bringing a pot of water to boil *and*

easily passing the egg. Sometimes it results from a depletion of nutrients due to laying too many eggs or raising too many broods in a short amount of time. A pair of vets have reported on one cockatiel hen who became egg bound after laying more than 40 eggs in a single month!

Egg binding is pretty easy to detect in most cases—the hen will sit with puffed-up feathers, closing her eyes and straining. If the egg has

Above: *The sheath in which a feather develops dries and eventually flakes off, allowing the feather to unfurl.*

turning it off before placing the bird above it. (We women can tell when the steam's the right temperature because it's comfortable enough for us to "sauna" our complexions by holding our faces over the pot.) A *small* amount of petroleum jelly may help lubricate the vent. A beginner

The range of pigments that an adult cockatiel will exhibit
become apparent with the first coat of feathers.

Common Breeding Problems

should never try to move the egg down the reproductive tract through massage or other external manipulation because the chances of breaking the egg are just too high. If steaming the vent doesn't result in expulsion of the egg, contact a vet right away. Immediate action can make the difference between life and death for the hen.

To prevent egg binding, don't overbreed your hens. Two or three broods a year is enough. Always have cuttlebone or another mineral source available to the hen, as well as good sources of vitamins A and D. Unlike humans, your cockatiel can't manufacture vitamin D from vegetable matter, so egg yolk or enriched protein food is vital. Since outdoor birds can make vitamin D from sunlight, using a full-spectrum fluorescent light indoors may also help prevent deficiencies. A good avian vitamin mix will help prevent problems. Since cockatiels don't drink very

Above: The bald area behind the crest is most pronounced in lutino cockatiels.

much water, the kind that you sprinkle on their food is most likely to get inside the birds.

A problem that really isn't a problem: You see your hen producing loose, watery droppings around egg-laying time. This phenomenon is perfectly normal and not uncommon.

Birds frequently lay some infertile eggs along with the fertile members of a clutch. However, if clutch after clutch is infertile, something is wrong with one of the parents. Since the cock must mount the hen to fertilize her eggs, a male with an amputated or deformed leg can't be expected to father young even if he's perfectly fine otherwise. Keep him as a pet, and find another male for

A lutino cockatiel housed in a spacious flight.

your breeding project. An overweight male can also have trouble touching his vent to the female's; in his case, slim him down by removing fatty seeds and restricting him to protein food, fruits, and vegetables. Insist that he exercise even if you must remove him from the cage yourself to get him out into the room. Another treatable cause of infertility occurs when an overgrowth of feathers obstructs the vent. Trim these feathers carefully and look for improvement. Poor nutrition may also lead to infertility in either or both parents.

Another problem that probably results from poor nutrition is fertile embryos dying in the shell after only a few days of development. If the hen can't give her babies all they need to grow and

Below: *Indoor breeding cages constructed of wire mesh are easy to maintain.*

develop within the shell, they have a real problem since they can't eat until they hatch! Again, plenty of protein and a good vitamin supplement should prevent most cases.

The very young hatchlings are quite sensitive to diseases that might not bother an older bird. If you must handfeed from day one, giving a drop or two of cultured yogurt for the first few feedings may provide the beneficial bacteria the babies need to fight infection. (If parent-raised, these bacteria will come from the regurgitated food fed by the parents.) You can't do much about cleaning the box once a brood is established, so make sure any nest box you offer is clean before putting it in with the birds, and clean it again after every brood finishes. Change the litter or lining of the brooder containing handfed birds at least once a day.

Not so hard, is it? At least, not when you consider the results—a healthy brood of beautiful and affectionate cockatiels!

Below: *A shipping container for birds has one side angled to ensure adequate ventilation if something is stacked atop it.*

A Cockatiel Aviary

Setting up an aviary or flight cage is a great way to make sure your cockatiels get enough exercise, and it can beautify your home or garden as well. However, before you plunge into the carpentry business, take the time to do some planning. A thoughtful arrangement can be a pleasure for both you and the birds, while a thrown-together hodge-podge can have the neighbors petitioning you to leave the neighborhood!

The first thing you must determine is whether you will have your aviary indoors or out. You will probably have

Above: *Cockatiels are peaceable enough to be housed with a wide variety of other species, such a doves.*

more room if you can expand into the outdoors, and your birds will have the benefit of getting their vitamin D, ''the sunshine vitamin,'' direct from the source. You will, of course, add to the beauty and interest of your garden. And, best of all, cockatiels get more exercise and breed

Chicken wire, though not ideal for an aviary, will not be damaged by a cockatiel's chewing.

A Cockatiel Aviary

more quickly and easily in a roomy outdoor aviary!

However, if you live in a suburban or urban neighborhood, watch out for zoning restrictions. A law meant to discourage backyard poultry may be interpreted as a ban on all bird keeping, while restrictions on commercial interests in residential neighborhoods have been used to persecute hobbyists who must occasionally sell excess stock. Your sweet, quiet cockatiels certainly won't bother anybody, but they can make a convenient target for cranks, so find out what the law is *before* you start pouring concrete.

Vandals and thieves are also a problem in suburban and urban areas. I have met uninformed individuals who didn't know the difference between a cockatiel and a cockatoo, but they certainly knew that one of the two can be worth hundreds of dollars! Indeed, I know of one theft where an ignorant teenager robbed an aviary and stole an inexpensive (but loved) pet parrot only to leave several macaws worth thousands of dollars apiece alone. In that case the owner got lucky—the boy's father returned the bird and refused the handsome reward offered by the owner—but why tempt fate? Plan to install a security system that includes both locks and alarms.

If you're in a rural location with a mild-to-moderate

climate, you're in the best position for an outdoor aviary for cockatiels. Defenses against winged and four-footed predators are relatively inexpensive and quite reliable, and you'll find housing the hardy, adaptable cockatiel much easier than caring for a fussy tropical bird. If you have the land in this situation, you really have no reason to deny yourself or your birds the pleasure of an outdoor aviary. Just watch out: This hobby's highly addictive! You may end up with flight pens sprouting across your ranch like mushrooms!

Although this book isn't the place for an in-depth carpentry lesson, let's quickly take a look at some of the things you'll need to know before you build. *Every* outdoor aviary should have a well-lit enclosed section that you can drive the birds into during bad weather. The door between the outdoor and indoor portions can be left open most of the time, so that the birds can come and go as they like; if you provide proper, comfortable perches and roosts, most of your cockatiels will probably also use this inner area for sleeping. Don't try to do without such a shelter even if you enjoy a mild climate. Do you really want your cockatiels getting blown about, say, during a hurricane? In more extreme climates, the shelter will need a heat source. A couple of infrared heat lamps placed

These cockatiels show some of the range of delicate colors possible by combining mutations.

Companions

near the roosting boxes are fine for a few tough guys like cockatiels, but if you have more delicate species housed with them, you may need something more elaborate. You must also cover part of the outdoor roof so that there is *always* shade to be found within the aviary. To prevent escapes, build a double-door "escape hatch" system. Although a variety of aviary shapes are possible, keep in mind that a *long* flight pen will be best for a strong flyer like the cockatiel.

A concrete aviary floor is easy to wash down and will protect against rodents, but it isn't as attractive or simple to care for as a natural earth floor, which often will renew itself unless you have overstocked it with birds. It also allows for natural planting, which will be especially appreciated by any cockatiel occupants of the aviary. If you plan on a dirt floor, be sure to sink the aviary sides in trenches at least 18 inches into the dirt. Rats and mice will probably not go that far down to break in, but an armadillo certainly might! Be aware of the pests in your area so you'll know what to guard against.

A greenhouse or indoor bird room is also a nice option. Some handy hobbyists have even converted spare closets into small, comfortable bird rooms. (Not me! At my house, there's no such thing as a spare closet!) The floor and walls should be

made of tile or other easily cleaned material, and the lighting should include full-spectrum fluorescents that are on 15 hours a day while the cockatiels are breeding. Plants in pots may be rotated in and out of the bird room to add a natural air without allowing an enthusiastic chewer a chance to gnaw anything to death.

Companions

Whether you opt for an outdoor flight or indoor bird room, you're unlikely to feel satisfied with a bare-bones set-up containing perches, nest-box, and cockatiels. (The cockatiels themselves, however, will thrive in such a situation.) You want a beautiful aesthetic experience out of all your hard work! So how can you turn a nice aviary into a little piece of Australian habitat?

Cockatiel-stuffing isn't the way. You will do best if you never keep more than one adult pair of cockatiels and their unweaned young to a flight. If cockatiel breeding is your main interest, you should build a flight, preferably 6 to 10 feet long, for *each* pair. Mixing many cockatiels can lead to nesting and territory disputes that cut down on breeding, and it prevents you from breeding superior offspring by controlling who mates with whom. Even if you did get a prize-winning specimen, you probably wouldn't be able to figure out which pair produced it so that

A normal-colored male cockatiel.

you could repeat your success! For these reasons, one flight, one pair remains the best rule unless you aren't breeding your birds.

Many other kinds of avian companions are perfectly fine and get along wonderfully with a cockatiel. Since cockatiels are gentle and unaggressive, you should go smaller rather than larger when choosing potential pals. Budgies, finches and canaries, and inoffensive ground-dwellers such as quail are good choices. Avoid lovebirds; they may look small and sweet, but they are bad sports about sharing with anyone but their mates. A

Above: *Outdoor aviaries are best furnished with natural perches.*

nice Australian grouping would consist of a pair each of cockatiels, zebra finches, and diamond doves. All three share similar habitats and are especially hardy in outdoor aviaries.

For a successful community aviary, you must provide sufficient feeders and water fonts, lots of cover, and above all, *room!* A small feeder for every pair of birds will prevent

In general, cockatiels are steady birds, whether faced with people or other birds.

a bully from keeping others from eating their fill. (I have witnessed pairs of tiny zebra finches chase pairs of the much larger button quails from feeders and even their own nests, so don't think it can't happen because you made such wise choices.) Cover should be supplied by safe vegetation. A corner stand of grass is especially well liked by Australian birds; small fruit trees, eucalyptus, and privet can also provide good munching as well as safe cover. Smaller plants should be on the tough side so that they'll survive the birds' attentions; for instance, bromeliads and palms are excellent southern choices. Be sure you aren't inadvertently choosing a poisonous plant to place in

Below: *The typical aviary consists of a flight area and a shelter room.*

with your birds!

If you have enough cover and feeders, but the birds are still fighting, you just haven't given them enough room. You have a serious problem on your hands. Territory disputes may seem "cute" and "funny"—until the day when one angry bird corners another and tears it apart. You can't blame the aggressor, since its hormones (especially during breeding) are telling it to clear its territory of competitors for mates, nesting areas, and food. It's up to you to make sure that each bird feels like it has more than enough room to be generous with others.

Be *very* conservative when making your plans. A finches-only aviary might have as many as 1 bird for every 10 cubic feet, but a cockatiels-only aviary should have *100* cubic feet for every bird if you're putting more than one pair to a flight. Obviously, you

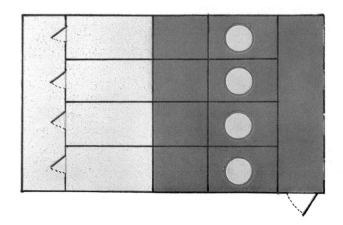

Above: *Increased room to fly is only one of the benefits of housing cockatiels outdoors.*

can decrease the birds' sense of territorial competition if you have only one pair of each species per flight, since different species fill different niches in nature; hence, a pair each of budgies, cockatiels, and finches could do very well in a moderately sized flight. Still, even restricting yourself to a pair of each different species, 1 bird for each 10 cubic feet is a good rule to follow. As you get acquainted with your own birds, you may find that you can get away with some more—or you may find you have to cull a few! Whenever you have personality clashes in the aviary, it's almost certainly a sign that you have too many birds in a confined space.

Got the picture now? Your perfect, peaceful dream aviary won't be cluttered with birds like the stuffed toy rack at the store. Instead, it will be a quiet, airy, natural environment where all have room to exercise, reproduce, and generally go about their business without harassment from others. If you're doing things right, you'll soon find yourself envying your birds' idyllic, uncrowded existence.

I said it before and I'll say it again: Never put a new bird in with your old birds! Always keep it separated from the others for a month unless you've gotten a vet's okay. It's always possible that even the most carefully chosen pet sold from the cleanest shop with the best intentions somehow picked up a disease that isn't showing yet. My favorite cliché applies: Better safe than sorry!

I've also said time and time again that cockatiels are tough, hardy birds, and that's

Above: *Medicines can be administered orally with an eye dropper.*

certainly true. Their history of domestication even before aviculture was a sophisticated study proves that. However, living in an unnatural environment will always produce some degree of stress in an animal, whether bird or human. If the situation is pleasantly challenging—you play with your pet often and teach it tricks—your bird experiences the positive

Slightly fluffed feathers may indicate relaxation before sleeping as well as the onset of illness.

Coping with Injuries and Illnesses

stress that prolongs its life while making it fun. If the situation is tedious, your cockatiel suffers the stress of boredom, which can lead to a feather-plucked suicide. If the situation is actively unpleasant, well, the poor bird probably won't be around very long to complain about it. That doesn't contradict my statement that cockatiels are hardy; it merely confirms the fact that very few birds of any kind will live, much less thrive, under poor conditions.

You, of course, care enough to read a book about caring for your pet. You wouldn't force your cockatiel to spend its days picking at moldy seed in a dinky cage coated with filth. But it's so easy to forget about the thing your pet cockatiel needs most of all: companionship. If your circumstances change so that you're too busy to play with a solitary pet, by all means find it a mate or even a new owner! The social interaction vital to the psychological health of these friendly birds is your number-one protection against disease and self-inflicted injury.

Treated well, a pet cockatiel is in a great position to enjoy many years of health. Especially if it has no contact with other birds, it has relatively little opportunity to acquire many disease organisms. The individual attention it gets from you is a plus that provides it with physical, as well as psychological, resilience. Yet, in this imperfect world, even the best-kept pet may be injured or stricken by disease. By preparing yourself in advance for an emergency, you can give your cockatiel the help it needs without fear or panic.

"A sick bird is a dead bird" is *not* true for cockatiels. Although no bird's illness should be treated lightly, you should remember that a good vet, especially one who specializes in birds, can frequently save a cockatiel's life. It's a good idea to locate an avian vet in advance. Get out your pencil right now and drop a line to the Association of Avian Veterinarians, P.O. Box 299, East Northport, NY 11731, requesting a list of members in your area. Although the association can't guarantee a member's expertise, you can certainly assume that a vet interested enough to join this organization cares about birds! Because avian science (other than poultry science) is so young, it may seem to you that your vet spends an awful lot of time looking up information in books or journals when working on your case. That's actually a good sign, not a bad one. There is no way that any vet could have learned all there is to know about the many pet birds in vet school when most of the findings are just being published now.

Getting to the vet shouldn't be a worry with a tame cockatiel. If its usual

Should a cockatiel become ill, tameness makes treatment easier to accomplish and less stressful to the cockatiel.

Above: *Pet cockatiels should occasionally be given a physical examination to detect any developing problems.*

emergency. In any event, be sure to cover the cage when moving the bird to give it privacy and to keep it warm during transport.

Coping with Illness

It isn't always easy to tell when a cockatiel is sick. All birds have a tendency to conceal illness, leftover from days in the wild when showing weakness was sure to attract a hungry predator in search of easy prey. Behavior changes are often the first sign of sickness in a cockatiel. If your bird loses interest in its usual games and surroundings, especially if its stops preening its feathers, it's probably sick. Other symptoms include weight loss, puffed-out feathers, and discharges from eyes, nostrils, or vent. Sometimes you won't realize how much weight a "puffy" bird has lost until you feel under its feathers and find that its keelbone sticks out like a sharp little knife.

You can treat your cockatiel at home if its symptoms aren't too severe. It's a good idea to keep on hand a smallish, long hospital cage for the convalescent's use so that it will be able to get to food and water without much effort. A heat lamp or light bulb should be placed at one end of the cage so that the cockatiel can seek extra warmth if needed. Since a bird's body temperature is *normally* close to 110°F, a bird with a fever can burn up its fuel reserves in a matter of hours! The

cage is portable, remove cups, toys, and all except for one perch to make moving it less stressful. Put a millet spray and a bit of fruit on the bottom of the cage so that your cockatiel can nibble should the urge strike, but don't clean the tray now; many vets like to look at the droppings to help diagnose the illness. If the cage isn't portable, you should transfer your pet into a small travel cage kept on hand in case of

The eyes are often a good indicator of health in a cockatiel: wide-open, bright eyes are a sign of well-being.

outside warmth will help prevent its body from exhausting itself. Place the cage in a secluded location so that the cockatiel will feel secure instead of self-conscious about others noticing that it's sick. The hospital cage is also excellent first aid until you can get in touch with a vet.

Many people successfully treat minor problems at home by combining the use of the hospital cage with a pet-shop or home remedy. However, you can't expect to diagnose avian disease yourself since many illnesses show the same symptoms. Only a vet or lab analysis will get to the root of some problems. If your pet doesn't respond to home care after a couple of days or if it takes a turn for the worse, get help immediately.

What about parrot fever? Don't worry. Although cockatiels and other parrots can certainly catch this disease, the name is a misnomer because they are not the major carriers. Pigeons, especially feral ones, are probably responsible for most of the spread of this disease. An indoor cockatiel has little chance of developing parrot fever, but if it does, it can be cured if given the proper treatment in time. In the unlikely circumstances that *you* catch parrot fever, you'll find that your doctor can cure you too. Of course, if you ever contract a mysterious ailment, you would tell your doctor that you keep a cockatiel so that he or she could test for the possibility, but certainly don't let fear of this curable disease deprive you of the pleasure of a cockatiel.

Coping with Injury

Cockatiels are resistant to disease, but are they accident prone! If something panics them, they fly, and if they're inside, they usually fly right into a wall. Most of the time, they'll bounce right back, but if they don't, having a home hospital cage on hand can be a real lifesaver.

If an injured cockatiel is bleeding, act fast! A bird doesn't have much blood to spare. Styptic powder can stop bleeding from a broken claw or feather; otherwise, apply direct pressure on a wound to stop bleeding. The heat from the hospital cage will help combat shock until you get the cockatiel to a vet for help. Later, it can be used with the lamp off to prevent the bird from moving too much until fully recovered. Don't despair. Broken wings and legs splinted by the vet *can* recover full function. Even if your curious cockatiel got so tangled up in something that its foot must be amputated, there's no reason to give up. Although unable to copulate, cockatiels with one leg can otherwise lead perfectly normal lives.

Sometimes a cockatiel gets in trouble coming in for a landing—if the place it has decided to land looks like a

In the home, a cockatiel is likely to fly to the highest perching place available.

nice cool bubbly bath and is actually a pot of boiling water! If its feet are scalded, flush them thoroughly with cold water and dry gently with sterile gauze. It won't feel much like moving for a while, so, once again, let it spend a few days in the hospital cage. A severe burn, of course, requires immediate attention from a vet. It's better to avoid this heartache by keeping lids on your cooking containers.

Because cockatiels like to chew, they may also eat some thing around the house that's not good for them. If an object is lodged in the crop, they won't be able to digest or eat again until it's removed.

Above: *Never allowing a cockatiel the freedom of a room unless it is supervised is one of the best ways to prevent accidents.*

See the vet at once. Always consider the possibility of poisoning if your cockatiel gets sick. Mention to the vet any plants, unusual foods, medications, ball-point pens, or anything else you've noticed the bird gnawing. Also mention if you've done any spraying for insects, or used any form of flea control or insecticide on a family cat or dog.

Hand-tame cockatiels are just as liable to have accidents as untame birds.

The coloration of lutino cockatiels makes distinguishing the sexes difficult.

Suggested Reading

ENCYCLOPEDIA OF COCKATIELS
by George A. Smith
(PS-743)

After placing the Cockatiel in the context of other parrots and relating the history of its domestication, Dr. Smith discusses it first as a pet: selection, care, taming, and talking. A chapter on behavior in the wild introduces the section on breeding, which covers accommodations, maintenance, the breeding cycle, and problems that may arise. Comments on each of the color varieties are succeeded by an exposition of the genetics involved. The final chapter deals with health maintenance. "If you needed to limit yourself to one book on cockatiels, this is the volume I would suggest." Arthur Freud in *American Cage-Bird Magazine*.
Illustrated with 60 color and 108 black-and-white photos. Hard cover, 5½ × 8', 256 pp.

ALL ABOUT BREEDING COCKATIELS
by Dorothy Bulger
(PS-801)

Discusses breeding Cockatiels, artificial incubation and head-rearing, hand-taming and talking, grooming and health problems, and adds helpful hints.
Illustrated with 30 color and 20 black-and-white photographs. Hard cover, 5½ × 8', 96 pp.

COCKATIEL HANDBOOK
by Gerald R. Allen and Connie Allen
(PS-741)

This authoritative handbook on keeping and breeding Cockatiels is the outgrowth of many years of study and observation by a husband-and-wife team living in Australia. Covering anatomy, natural history, pet care, and diseases and illnesses.
Illustrated with 77 color and 96 black-and-white photos. Hard cover, 5½ × 8', 256 pp.

EXPERIENCES WITH MY COCKATIELS
by Mrs. E. L. Moon
(AP-1280)

Tells how the Lutino mutation in Cockatiels was established, along with other tales about Cockatiel keeping.
Illustrated with 28 color and 41 black-and-white photographs. Hard cover, 5½ × 8', 128 pp.

PARROTS OF THE WORLD
by Joseph M. Forshaw
(PS-753)

Every species and subspecies of parrot in the world, including those recently extinct, is covered in this authoritative work. Almost 500 species or subspecies appear in the color illustrations by William T. Cooper. Descriptions are accompanied by distribution maps and accounts of behavior, feeding habits, and nesting.
Almost 300 color plates. Hard cover, 9½ × 12½', 584 pp.

Index

Page numbers set in **boldface** type refer to illustrations.